Green Cheeked Conure.

Green Cheek Conures as pets.

Green Cheek Conures Keeping, Pros and Cons, Care, Housing, Diet and Health.

by

Roger Rodendale

GW00498753

Table of Contents

Introduction

Green cheek conures are among the most popular pet birds, and for good reason. These birds are extremely goofy and can be quite entertaining. You can watch these birds for hours, as they perform several antics like hanging from the bars of their cage or just climbing on their favorite perches.

Green cheek conures are also great pets because they love to play. Once they are used to you, they will also let you cuddle and pet them quite a bit. You can lay the birds on their back and give them a good rub on the belly. This is not something that all birds will let you do.

These birds are also perfect for anyone who is looking at breeding conures. Since they breed very easily in captivity, they make the perfect choice for you. They are good for those who are just starting to breed birds. If you have some experience with birds, you can even breed interesting color mutations.

In addition to all of this, these birds are extremely beautiful to look at. They have bright green plumes that are distinct and very pleasing to the eyes. So, if you are looking for a pet that will be extremely affectionate and is also great to show off, the green cheek conure is your best bet.

These birds hail from South America. They normally dwell in the canopies of the beautiful rainforests of this tropical region. That said, they have very specific needs when it comes to food and care. Therefore, you need to have ample information available at your disposal when you decide to bring one of these birds home.

This book will tell you everything that you need to know about raising conures. It covers various subjects like:

- Helping your bird make the transition into your home
- Training the bird
- Bonding with your bird
- Correct healthcare
- Housing
- Maintenance of the bird
- Breeding.

This is your go-to guide if you are still a beginner and do not have any experience with pet birds. It is also a great reference for those who have some experience with other species of birds but not conures.

All the information provided in this book is practical and easy to understand. That way, when your conure is home you will know exactly what he needs to be happy and healthy.

Note: some people call this conure Green Cheek Conure and others Green Cheeked Conure. You will find both throughout this book.

Chapter 1: Introduction to Green Cheek Conures

Green cheek conures are small sized parrots that also go by the name Green cheek parakeet. Usually in aviculture or in pet stores, people refer to this bird as a conure, although there are different varieties of the conure.

Since the green cheeked conure is the most common one of all, this bird represents the name conure. These birds belong to the genus *Pyrrhura*. This is the genus that all long-tailed parrots fall into. These parrots are new world parrots.

Typically, green cheeked conures are 26 cms in length. They are small birds weighing between 60 to 80 grams. The coloration of the bird is the most interesting thing. For the most part, conures are green in color.

The color of the crown varies between black, brown, and grey. They have a white ring around their eyes. The primary wing feathers are blue in color. The beak is grey in color. The tail is pointed and is mostly maroon in color. The breast has transverse striations that are short and even. The abdominal area is red in color. Both male and female are identical in appearance.

However, there are small differences that will help you tell the male and female apart.

1. Differentiating between male and female conures

Many experts will tell you that DNA sexing is the best way to tell the difference between a male and female green cheek. This is true because conure male and female birds look extremely similar. While this is the most reliable test, there are also some minute differences in structure and color that you can use to tell them apart.

The feet

This is one of the lesser known facts about green cheek conures. Most female green cheek conures have pink colored feet. In most cases, the male birds have grey feet. Although this may vary, for the most part, the feet are differently colored.

Remember, going only by the color of the feet is not a good idea. There are also chances of mutations in the bird that can lead to different colored feet. While this is one method, it certainly is not the best one around.

Shape of the head

The head of a female conure is normally soft and more rounded. In the case of the male conures, the head is flat at the crown. While there are a few exceptions depending on each individual bird, this method has proven to be useful in several cases to determine the gender of conures.

Pelvis examination

This is a method that is normally used by breeders. They will check to see if it is a female or a male before the bird is sold. Hold the bird in your hand gently, then feel the breast bone of the bird. Just before the cloaca of the bird, the breast bone seems to split. If it does split, then it is a female conure.

This is because the hip bones are wider in the case of females because they need to lay eggs. In the case of males, this structure is closer and you will not be able to feel the split physically. Therefore, in case of the male, the structure is seemingly sharper.

DNA Sexing

All of the methods mentioned above are useful but not 100% accurate. When you are looking for a mate for your bird or when you have a particular gender you want to bring home, for varied reasons, DNA sexing is the most sure shot way of making your decision.

Your bird can be taken to the vet for DNA sexing. Two methods are normally used; blood DNA sexing or feather DNA sexing. Veterinary surgery is also carried out but it is not advisable to put your bird through the stress only to determine its gender.

2. Different color mutations of green cheek conures

Green cheek conures are extremely popular in aviculture. Since the rise in their demand, several breeders have begun to create new varieties of these birds. These birds are among the most colorful conures and certain genetic mutations have led to interesting plumage and coloration.

Today, there are six sub species of these birds that are identified based on their color. Knowing in detail about each specific type will help you decide which one you want to bring home. The six types of green cheek conures are:

a) Regular or "normal" green cheeks: These are the most common type of green cheek conures. They retain the original coloration of the birds that were first identified in the wild.

How they look: These birds have green wing feathers and grey feathers on the chest. The tail is red in color. In the case of these birds, there is no sign of yellow on the chest. They tend to have grey feet.

There is another slight variation of these birds called the pied green cheek conures. They may have a few feathers on the chest that are red or yellow. However, they do not have enough of them and can thus be differentiated from a yellow-sided green cheek conure.

Personality: These birds are very similar to the yellow cheeked conures in terms of personality. They are extremely fun loving birds that can even be goofy at times. They will keep you entertained with antics like hanging upside down from the cage and bathing in the water bowls.

These birds are mostly independent and can keep themselves entertained for the most part. However, they do need your attention from time to time, as without it they may develop behavioral issues. However, unlike the bigger species of parrots, they will do quite fine by themselves when you have to leave them and go off to work, for instance.

How to breed them: These are the easiest birds to breed. You can breed a male green cheek with a female of the same subspecies. Cross breeding is not necessary.

Cost of buying: If you buy these birds from a breeder, they may cost between $175-$200. Pet stores are usually about 10% higher in cost.

b) Yellow-sided green cheek conure

How they look: They have green wing feathers with blue tips. The tail is red in color. The distinctive feature of this mutation is the bright red and yellow plumage on the chest instead of grey like the normal green conures. The head feathers are grey or black in color. Unlike normal conures, these birds have pink feet.

Personality: Just like normal green cheek conures, these birds are also extremely fun loving. They are also very fond of snuggling with their owners. After a good nap, they will keep you entertained with their antics.

These birds are extremely independent. This means that you do not have to feel any pangs of guilt for leaving them at home while you are at work. The only behavioral issue noticed with these birds is that they are quite nippy when they are young. You can train them to stop doing this.

How to breed them: Breeding yellow sided conures is not hard. You can breed a pair of these birds to get the exact offspring. All you need are the right nesting conditions.

Cost of buying: These birds are a tad bit more expensive than the regular green cheek conures. They usually cost between $200-225 when you buy them from a private breeder.

c) Cinnamon green cheek conures

How they look: These birds have a much lighter feather coloration. The wings are light green in color and have a few light blue feathers. They look dull in coloration in comparison to the regular green cheek conures. The bean is tan or brown in color. The head also has tan feathers, unlike other mutations, which have black or grey feathers.

The chest coloration is very similar to the yellow-chested green cheek conures. It is bright yellow and red in color.

Personality: In comparison to the yellow-sided and the normal green cheek conures, these birds are more independent. These birds are shy and are more cautious in comparison. They are not very quick to shower their affection and will only do so when they get used to you.

8

These birds prefer to be left alone in their cage. They are not exactly fond of playing outside the cage. Only when they warm to you and get entirely comfortable will they entertain any play. These birds are also moody in comparison to other types of green cheek conures.

How to breed them: These birds are also easy to breed and do not require any cross breeding. However, for breeding to be successful these birds require a lot of good food and ideal nesting conditions. They also need a lot of peace and quiet to lay their clutches.

Cost of buying: When you buy them from a private breeder, these birds cost about $175-$200.

d) Pineapple green cheek conure

How they look: These birds have very bright colors on their body. The chest is red and yellow in color. The wings are bright green and red. The head also has bright yellow and red colors. These birds are extremely rare and are quite distinct from the rest of the green cheek mutations. The colors on this bird make it look quite similar to a ripe pineapple.

Personality: These birds are the result of breeding cinnamon green cheek conures and yellow-sided green cheek conures, so they have the best personality traits of them both. They are more fun loving in comparison to the yellow sided conures. However, they are perfectly okay on their own.

These birds are slightly cautious like the cinnamon green cheek conure. However, they are quick to show affection and become extremely friendly.

How to breed them: Breeding these birds is a little tricky. These birds are the result of a recessive gene that is found in yellow-sided conures and cinnamon conures. Those who wish to breed these birds need to look for bright coloration and certain patterns in coloration.

When you are unsure of what to look for in the birds you choose to breed, you end up having a green cheek with a brighter yellow coloration or a regular yellow-sided green cheek conure.

It is not good enough to breed one pineapple conure with another either. Since the coloration is the result of recessive genes, you will end up having either fully red chicks or ones that are fully yellow in color. You have the option of buying a proven pair of pineapple green conures. These are birds that have hatched true pineapple conures in the past.

Cost of buying: These are among the rarest and the most expensive. You will have to shell out about $300-$350 when you buy one from a private breeder. In a pet store, the cost is much higher.

e) Turquoise green cheek conure

How they look: Blue green cheek conures are very rare. They have a sapphire wing hue that makes them the most wanted of all conure mutations. The tail is a dull burgundy color and the base is off-white. The head is a blue glowing hue, which matches the beak.

On average, turquoise green cheeks have grey down feathers on the chest. The stomach feathers are sapphire in color. There are other mutations that have feathers of different colors such as violet, azure, black, ruby, orange, and green on the chest.

Personality: These birds are the felines of the bird world. They are very standoffish and prefer to be by themselves. They have a lot of poise and dignity and are not very generous with showing affection. They may snuggle with you and play with you; however, they will also give you a quick nibble to tell you when they are done.

How to breed them: Breeding these birds is quite straight forward. You will have to find a breeder who is adept at breeding these birds and will be able to give you show quality turquoise conures. The rule of thumb is that the brighter the blue plumes, the better the babies are going to be.

Cost of buying: These birds are extremely rare, which also makes them highly expensive. You will be able to find them at prices above $400 even with a private breeder.

f) Ghost or muted green cheek conures

How do they look: These birds have a mint feather coloration. They are almost monochromatic with very few patches of light blue feathers on the stomach, tail, chest, head, and flight feathers.

Personality: These birds are known to be very meek and gentle. In fact, they have the sweetest personality of all the green cheek

10

conures. They can be skittish and shy in the beginning but once they get to know you, they are the most affectionate of them all. These birds are very similar to cockatoos in their personality and are as affectionate and attached to their owners.

However, they do not have the behavioral issues that are commonly associated with cockatoos. You will not have issues like feather picking with these birds.

How to breed them: These are very complex to breed and will require a breeder with ample experience. These birds are a cross between cinnamon green cheek conures and turquoise green cheek conures. The biggest issue with these birds is the possibility of the offspring developing strange behavioral traits.

Cost of buying: These birds will cost above $450 with a private breeder.

3. Natural habitat and range

Green cheek conures are seldom associated with the wilderness. Since these birds are so commonly bred in captivity, they are solely viewed as birds meant for aviaries.

These birds are native to the rain forest. In countries outside of South America, these birds are descendants of wild parrots that have been imported to a particular country.

These birds were originally found in South America. Even today, they are only found here in the wild. A major portion of the habitat of these birds belongs to Bolivia. They may also be found in some neighboring countries around Bolivia such as Argentina, Brazil, and Paraguay.

Typically, green cheek conures are found in marshy wetlands and dense forests. These birds actually cover a large range, which makes it very hard to specify the habitat of these birds. For instance, some of these birds are seen in the Andes flying 9000 ft high while others have been found making nests in the wetlands. They are even found in the Savannahs in some cases.

One common thing about all the habitats chosen by these birds is that they belong to the tropical zone. This is where the birds thrive the most.

In the wild, it is common to find large flocks of green cheek conures. They will only break away in pairs when the breeding season begins in order to raise their little ones. Once the babies have been weaned, the pair will return to the original flock. This is a cycle that has been followed by these birds for thousands of years.

Being in large flocks also offers these birds a great deal of security. They have also made adaptations to make sure that they are safe. To begin with, the coloration of these birds makes it very hard to find them when they are perching in the canopy of the rainforests. They are not even spotted by birds of prey that have very sharp vision.

These birds prefer to stay in taller trees, as predators will find it harder to get to them. This is one of the reasons why they build nests only on high trees. That way, predators will not be able to reach up and get the eggs.

In any case, these birds have very few predators because they are so hard to find. One of the predators is the false vampire bat. These birds are vulnerable to attacks by this predator only at night, however. Therefore, they escape most attacks as they are diurnal birds and will stay close to their nests at nightfall.

Another predator is the ornate hawk eagle. This eagle is possibly the biggest threat to these birds. Even so, they are hard to catch. Conures nest in areas where other bird species also nest. That way, any attack that the eagle prepares for gives the conure flock ample time to escape.

In the wild, green cheek conures live up to 30 years. This lifespan is reduced by almost 10 years when they are held in captivity. This is because of negligent owners who do not care for the birds properly.

4. Personality of the Green Cheek Conure

Green cheek conures are birds with big personalities. They are very interactive and highly intelligent. Like any other species of birds, there are some positives and some negatives to green cheek conures when it comes to behavior. Knowing them all will help you decide if these birds are ideal for you or not. (Please note: although there are females, from now on we shall refer to them as "he" for ease).

Best personality traits

There are some personality traits of conures that you will often compare with other parrots. There are four such traits that are often considered a positive when it comes to making the decision of buying the bird.

Cuddliness

- These birds are extremely similar to their large cousins, the macaws. This makes them quite cuddly and prone to showing affection.
- The amount of cuddliness depends on each individual bird.
- They like to have their head and neck petted.
- You can also lay them on their backs and give them belly rubs.
- Some green cheek conures will set boundaries with respect to affection.
- There are some who just may not like to be touched.

Playfulness

- These birds live to play.
- You can include several store bought and homemade toys for play.
- They love to climb and chew.
- One of the favorite activities of this bird is to hang upside down from the cage bars.
- They like to play games like picking up things you drop, wrestling, and lots more.

Curiosity

- These birds are a good mix of extremely outgoing birds and extremely cautious ones.
- Some birds may have phobias and might give into flight instincts.
- Socializing a green cheek conure will go a long way in determining how they interact with people.

Intelligence

- These birds are extremely intelligent.
- They seem to have a mind of their own.

- They have a high obedience/intelligence quotient, which makes them extremely easy to train.

Worst personality traits

While these birds are mostly a lot of fun and extremely entertaining, there are some personality traits that require some getting used to. They may be hard for you to handle if you are not entirely prepared for it.

Aggression

- Nippiness is one of the biggest problems with green cheek conures.
- These birds have large personalities and will do whatever it takes to get their way.
- If you do not interact with the bird and hand train them, they will nip at just about anything that comes towards them.
- These personality traits are most common with birds that are not sold properly at pet stores.
- The aggression can manifest itself in a variety of situations. Jealousy is one of them. The bird may attack someone approaching you while he is perched on your shoulder or hand.

Fearfulness

- For birds that have some traits of aggression, it is wrong to ignore the possibility of this behavior stemming from fear.
- If your conure is not socialized properly, he will develop a fear of human beings.
- They will show some amount of general fear towards anything that is unfamiliar to them. This is quite common.
- They may also show object fear, which is directed towards a particular object that is too brightly-colored or makes loud noises.
- If your bird shows fearful behavior towards certain objects, avoid bringing those objects around him.

Destructiveness

- Every parrot tends to be destructive to some degree.
- Conures are destructive because they are curious by nature.

- Green cheek conures, however, are the least destructive of all conure species.
- They will chew wood, paper, or just about anything that can be ripped apart.
- They need to be kept away from things you do not want them to chew.

Do they bond with just one person?

It is common for parrots to bond strongly with one person in the family. Then, they will only show affection to that one person and will long for their attention.

When this happens they may become fearful of other people or may even show signs of aggression towards them. However, as a general rule, green cheek conures and other birds classified as Pyrhurras are less prone to being one person birds.

This is because of their behavior in the wild. They prefer to stick to their flock and are usually very social. These birds, however, are monogamous and will have just one mate for life. As a result, they may bond strongly with one person and view them as the mate. That does not stop them from allowing other people to handle them as long as they are well socialized.

Green cheek conures and kids

Green cheek conures are good family birds, as they love to play. They like to be touched or handled. Other species of parrots such as cockatiels are less comfortable when they are handled.

However, when it comes to children, it is recommended that you are cautious. Most conures go through a nippy phase when they are younger. This may be dangerous for a child. In addition to that, children can become overly affectionate and may make the bird uncomfortable. If the child pulls or yanks on the feathers, they can respond aggressively.

In general, parrots are great family birds. However, there are very few species that are recommended for homes with children.

Single bird or a pair?

Having two birds can be a good thing and a bad thing. On a positive note, when they become good friends, these birds will keep each other company. That means you will not have to pay much attention

15

to the birds. Given their general nature, conures will still like to be handled by you and will give you some affection too.

On the negative side, if the birds do not get along with each other, it can be a nightmare. This will require you to keep them away from each other or even house them separately. This will mean that you have to give the birds twice the amount of attention as you would with one bird.

In some cases, birds that are not great together when housed in one cage will still be able to spend some time playing with one another when they are outside the cage. Even in this case, you will have to make ample time for both birds.

The best option when you decide to bring home more than one bird is to bring pair bonded birds. These birds are always going to love each other's company. They will, however, not want any attention from you. They may even not like to be handled by the owners. That said, they are still going to make entertaining pets.

When you have a pair bonded bird, you also have to make the crucial decision of whether you want them to breed or not. If you do want the birds to breed, you will have to make sure that you do not give them the nesting conditions that they will require. If not, you have to be prepared to raise the young birds properly.

Chapter 2: Finding a Green Cheek Conure

Green cheek conures are extremely popular pets. This is one of the main reasons why there are so many options for you to buy one and bring one home. However, not all of these sources are legal. Most of them may also sell you poorly bred birds that may develop several health issues.

In this chapter, we will discuss in detail all the available sources to buy a green cheeked conure so that you can choose the most legitimate and humane option.

1. Choosing a breeder

With the bird becoming a common household pet, several breeders have popped up over the years. Some of them are genuine hobby breeders who look for the best varieties of birds before breeding them. These breeders also ensure that the birds are kept in the best state of health.

The first step to bringing home a green cheeked conure is to find the perfect breeder. Here are a few tips that will be of great assistance:

- Look for a local breeder who works in an area that is conveniently located from your home.

- You can get a list of breeders on the internet. You can even look for advertisements about birds for sale in the classifieds section of your local newspaper.

- When you find a listing that seems genuine, you can contact them.

- The internet however is your best bet. You can find several breeder directories that will list the options available in your city and locality.

- Look for details of local bird groups and clubs online. You will also be able to meet several other conure owners in these clubs who can be very valuable in providing you with information and assistance with your pet.

17

- Ask for recommendations from conure owners or from people who own parrots. You can get a firsthand account from them about their experiences with various breeders.

- Besides conure clubs, you can even look for clubs that work towards the protection and conservation of exotic birds. These clubs are extremely passionate about learning about conures and other exotic birds. They also take great responsibility in ensuring that the birds are bred correctly. These clubs will only connect you with the best and most reliable breeders in your city. They may even help you raise your conure properly.

Once you have found a breeder who looks promising, make sure you visit their facility. Although several breeders have websites and an active online presence, remember that seeing is believing. When you visit the facility, you will get a good idea about the breeding practices and the intentions of the breeder.

The first interview with your breeder is crucial to understand whether or not he is the right person to buy your conure from. You can ask the breeder the following questions to get a good idea about their husbandry methods and breeding practices:
- How much experience do they have with breeding and raising green cheeked conures?
- Are the birds hand reared?
- What are the birds fed?
- How often are the birds bred each year?
- Do they have an avian vet they can recommend?

A genuine breeder will be interested to answer any questions that you have. These breeders genuinely care about their birds. They will be able to provide you with answers instantly and confidently.

A good breeder takes great pride in his/her facility. S/he will want to show you how the birds are raised and will know a lot about each bird that you are shown. The enthusiasm of the breeder is a great quality to look for.

As you converse with the breeder, you will get a fair idea of their interests. A good breeder will be eager to share every bit of information that s/he has about green cheeked conures. On the other hand, if the breeder is making excuses to show you the aviary or the other areas at the facility, it is a red flag.

If you notice any hesitation in providing answers to your questions, it means that the breeder is mostly looking at the commercial interest in breeding and raising conures. The breeders should be eager to tell you more about the bird. However, if their only point of interest is making a sale, then look for more options.

The breeder that you choose is not only crucial for you to obtain birds that are healthy, but can also become a great source of information when you face any challenges when it comes to raising your beloved pet.

The next thing you need to make sure is that you check the facility thoroughly before you buy a bird. The best kind of aviary is a closed one. Here, quarantining and sanitation is of utmost importance.

When you are going around the facility and taking a look around, there are some things that you need to keep an eye on:

- Make sure the cages are clean. There should not be any feces on the floor or in the food bowl. The floor and the food bowls should be free from feathers and feather dust to a good extent. In general, the cage should not look unkempt. Any good breeder will make sure that the birds are kept in a healthy and clean environment. This is a sign that the birds are at a lesser risk of diseases and infections.

- The food should be of good quality. Make sure that the birds are not restricted to a seed or pellet diet. For conures, having a large variety of foods is a must. A peek into the food bowl should reveal some fresh produce as well. If not, you will have to first introduce the bird to a good diet once you bring him or her home. That can be a challenge.

- The appearance of the birds also plays a very important role. Normally, like any other parrot, green cheeked conures are very alert and curious. If the bird stays on the floor of the cage or seems to back away into a corner when you approach him, it is a sign that he is not comfortable being around people. This may imply that he is not hand raised. In addition to that, the bird may also have health issues. Buying birds that are not friendly or are seemingly sick is certainly not a good idea. This is a sign that you have to look for other options.

When you have found a breeder who makes you comfortable enough to make a purchase, you can negotiate the sales terms. If the bird is still being hand trained or if the breeder has some special conditions for the purchase, you will not be able to take the bird home immediately. Some breeders insist that you spend some time with the bird before you take him home.

When you are waiting for the breeder to give you a clearance to take the bird home, you can make all the necessary preparations. This means you will have enough time to set up the cage of the bird, buy the toys, stock up on food and also get your family prepared. If you have everything ready for the bird to move in, then you will reduce a lot of stress on the part of the bird.

Does the breeder offer follow-up services?
The breeder should be able to provide good follow-up services. This is usually a part of the contract. If it is not, you may want to request the breeder for this service. You see, raising a conure is not as easy as putting him in a cage and feeding him. These birds are extremely complex and you are bound to have several questions and issues that you need to deal with along the way. A follow-up service will ensure that your breeder will help you find solutions to these problems.

Your green cheek conure will go through various stages of mental and physical development. You need an experienced breeder to help you through these stages and explain what is happening as each stage is occurring. The follow-up service is a great way to help you keep your bird as healthy as he can be. You will learn techniques to help your bird through the development stages. This ensures that he does not develop physical or mental illnesses. Ask your breeder if he or she is willing to support you. Most of them will be glad to help you, while others may not be that thrilled.

Ask for a health certificate
Whenever you buy a bird from a breeder, insist on getting a health certificate. This guarantees the fact that your bird is in good health. Usually, a good breeder will give you a health certificate by default.

When you get a health certificate, you need to have your bird examined in 72 hours by an avian vet for it to be valid. In case there are any genetic conditions or other health issues that are detected during this examination, you can return the bird. Even if the health issues are not detected immediately, you have 90 days to observe the bird. During this time, if there are any noticeable health issues, you can return the bird.

However, you need to make sure that your bird is properly quarantined in this period. This is even more important if you have other birds in your home. There are usually some conditions or rules associated with health certificates as follows:

- The pet owner must have the bird checked by an avian vet in less than 72 hours after purchase. In this checkup, if any health condition, genetic or otherwise, is discovered, the breeder will give you a replacement.

- Any health issue that develops due to poor sanitation or nutrition in the given time span is not the responsibility of the breeder or the pet store.

- These stores or breeders will not pay for any veterinary costs including the first checkup. In fact, the first time you may have to approach a vet who has been suggested by the breeder or the pet store for the checkup to be valid. This is not a good sign, as the vet and the breeder may be in cahoots in the entire process.

- Any accident or unfortunate incident will not be covered under this health guarantee.

The health guarantee only certifies that the bird that leaves the breeder or the pet store is in perfect condition. If there are any complications that develop under your care, you are solely responsible. Therefore, you need to make sure that you learn everything that you need to about these birds.

Certificate of Veterinary Inspection

If your birds are being shipped from the breeder's place or the pet store, make sure that you ask for a certificate of veterinary inspection. These certificates, also known as official health certificates, are necessary to ensure that your bird is not carrying any disease. These certificates are necessary in most states in the USA and in some parts of UK as well. These certificates are necessary when birds or any other livestock is entering a state for:

- A short visit
- Educational or research purposes
- Veterinary care
- A show or exhibition
- Sale as pets.

If you fail to get this certificate for your bird, chances are that he will not be allowed to pass customs. This experience can be stressful for the bird because there will be a lot of waiting and inspection that these birds absolutely hate. You must also check if your bird needs any permit to be brought into your state.

2. Consider adoption

Another great option to source your green cheek conure is to adopt a bird. There are several cases when green cheeked conures are left with rescue shelters because the owners are unable to take good care of it, because they are unable to handle certain behavioral issues or simply because they are moving to another town or city and the bird cannot go with them.

Since green cheek conures are common pets, you will find them in large numbers in local rescue shelters that house birds. However, if it is your first time with a pet bird, you may want to think twice before choosing to adopt.

The process of adoption is not as simple as going to the shelter and picking up a bird that you like. It is a lengthy process that requires you to show a lot of commitment towards the bird.

In some shelters, you will not have to pay anything to bring the bird home. In other cases, you may have to pay a basic adoption fee that covers the medical expenses of the bird.

When it comes to adoption, there are two options; you can either approach a rescue or you can approach a shelter. While they may seem like the same thing, they are quite different in reality.

How to adopt from a shelter
A shelter is a facility that is run by the local government or by a non-profit organization. These are public facilities such as the pound and animal control. Of course, there are some private facilities as well. These are usually referred to as humane societies or clubs. They usually have more branches.

These shelters are either government funded or are run by individuals or a group of people. Shelters work like an organization and have dedicated staff and even fixed working hours. There are also several volunteers who assist with adoption and general operations at these facilities.

You can look for sources to adopt your bird from online. There are dedicated websites that will give you details about the closest shelters to your home. They will also give you details on the birds that are available at these shelters.

With most of these shelters, the number of volunteers and staff is very low. That is why calling them to make enquiries may not be the best idea. Instead, you should visit them during their working hours. The details of the working hours are generally provided on the official website of each of these shelters. The websites will also list the birds that are up for adoption. If you can spot a green cheek conure among them, the next thing to do is to visit the shelter.

The procedure for adoption varies from one shelter to the other. The overall process is quite similar, however. Some rules that you need to be aware of before you adopt a pet bird are:

- The first step is to find a bird that you would like to adopt. Go through the listings provided by the website of the shelter.

- Paying a visit to the shelter to see the bird is a must. There is usually a reception desk at each shelter where you can get all the details of the bird that you want. You can even interact with the bird for a while to understand the personality and the temperament of the bird in general.

- You may have to pay an adoption fee in some shelters. This fee ranges from $20-$100 or £5-£50. It is entirely dependent on the shelter that you plan to adopt from. In addition, the more medical attention the bird may need after rescuing him, the higher the fees. This is primarily to ensure that any medical attention that is needed for the bird is covered.

- Once you have decided upon the bird that you want to take home, you will have to give them a valid ID. Shelters also have a mandatory house check. With exotic species like the green cheek conure, illegal trading and breeding is always a threat. These house checks are mandatory to ensure that the bird is going to a good home. The goal is to prevent any chance of trauma if the bird needs to be rescued again and has to go through the whole process all over again.

- You will have to complete the necessary paperwork. This will include details of vaccination and will also provide other health records of the bird.

- Make sure you spend some time with the bird before you decide to bring him or her home.

How to adopt from a rescue center
The term rescue refers to an individual bird that has been rescued by someone and is currently under their care. These birds can also be cared for in a private boarding facility. Some facilities are run by volunteers and have regular adoption events.

When looking for listings for adoption, a rescue listing can be contacted immediately. You can even set up a meeting. If it is a private boarding set up, you will have to fill out applications and complete their adoption procedure.

Some rules that apply to rescues include:

- You can send an email or connect with the rescue with the contact details provided. Rescues are quick to respond and will call you immediately.

- You will have to provide all the necessary details about yourself. You can get all the details about the bird that you want to rescue through this conversation.

- When you are sure that you can handle the responsibility of the bird, you can visit the shelter or one of their adoption events.

- A home check is necessary when you adopt from a rescue center. Only when the rescue is convinced that your house is a suitable environment for the bird will you be able to adopt.

- Once you are chosen to adopt the bird, you will have to submit all the necessary proof of ID. You will be handed over the health reports of the bird as well.

- In the case of an adoption contract, it has to be signed and the adoption fee should be paid. This fee is between $100-$300 or £50-150.

What you need to know about adopted conures
Adoption is a great option. Several parrots, including small ones like green cheek conures, are rescued each day. Some of these birds are injured, some are abandoned, and some are even abused. If you are willing to bring a green cheek conure that needs a loving family home, it is the noblest thing to do. However, there are some things that you need to know about adopting a pet bird:

- **The bird may be infected:** Birds, large or small, carry several infectious microbes that infect people as well. Avian tuberculosis and chlamydiosis can be transmitted to people through the air. This leads to several illnesses that can be serious, especially if people have a pre-existing health condition such as a weak immune system. Stressed birds also shed a lot of feather dust. This can lead to breathing problems. You need to have a HEPA air filter if you want to control any allergies related to bird feather dust.

- **The bird may have behavioral issues:** Remember, the parrot that you bring home may have gone through some terribly traumatic experiences. This means that the bird may be hard to handle. They may have extreme trust issues. They are highly intelligent birds. Now this is a disadvantage because they are able to remember their past experiences and will even form relationships based on this. These birds may exhibit behavior such as aggression and extreme fear. You need to be very patient with them.

- **You will have to invest more:** Many people adopt pets because they do not want to spend as much as they would if they were to buy a bird. If you are one of them, then you need to understand that rehabilitating the bird is far more expensive than its market value. You will have to take the bird to the vet often. In the case of any serious health conditions, you may have to spend hundreds of dollars on providing the right care for these birds. So, bring a bird home only if you are sure that you can afford all of these expenses.

- **You need to have time:** When a bird has lost trust, it requires a lot of training and effort from the owners to regain that trust. So, you will have to increase the interactions with the bird. You will need to make sure that you have the time to take him for all the veterinary appointments. You also need a lot of patience and time to keep trying to get the bird back to its normal, cheerful self. If you cannot give a bird that sort of time, avoid adoption.

- **They are harder to train:** It is likely that you will adopt an adult bird. These birds already have several habits that are hard to break. They would also have a fully developed personality. There may be specific things that they like and dislike. Therefore, it takes conscious effort from your end to ensure that you try to understand the personality of the bird that you brought home and take good care of him accordingly.

Adopting a bird is a lot harder than you can imagine, so it is better that you have some experience raising birds before you make this commitment.

3. Buying from pet stores

Not all pet stores are bad, but there are several stores that encourage commercial breeding practices that are not healthy for the birds. However, some of them are run by passionate individuals who are interested in breeding certain green cheek conure species. They may be interested in increasing awareness about these birds and the joy of having them as pets. You will know that a pet store could be buying from commercial breeders or, even worse, illegally smuggling them by the following signs:

- **The aviary is extremely noisy**: Conures stay close to their flocks in the wild. They need the companionship of their flock mates for their wellbeing. When they are separated from this flock after being captured, they still call out to them very loudly. For several days after they are separated from their flock, these birds continue to cry out to their fellow birds.

  Loneliness is one of the biggest issues with birds like this. Besides becoming very noisy, these birds can become aggressive and could even develop issues like feather plucking. That is when the birds begin to look unhappy and unkempt. In a good pet store, birds are usually bred in captivity. They are close to their flocks or sometimes even their parents. If the bird has no flock mate, the owners and the employees in the store take the additional effort to become their flock by spending a lot of time with them and keeping them mentally and physically active.

- **The birds are afraid of people:** Pet stores that care for the well being of their birds will spend a lot of time with them to make sure that they feel loved. Quite obviously, these birds are very well socialized and will be more approachable. On the other hand, if the birds have been smuggled in or have not been given the attention that they need, they will be aggressive or afraid. Most often, birds that have been smuggled in will relate to people as a threat to their well being. As a result, when you approach their cage or try to interact with them, they may just retreat to a corner of the cage. Some of them become defensive and will puff up their feathers or nip at you as an attempt to scare you away. These are the signs that tell you that the bird may be a difficult one to bring home, as you will have to deal with several behavioral problems.

- **The employees have no clue about the birds they are selling:** Talk to the employees at the pet store. It is not enough that just the pet store owner has all the information about the birds. The caretakers will be aware of the routine and the requirements of the birds if they have been interacting with them regularly. On the other hand, if they have to work with new species that are just smuggled in or bought from breeders, they may not be able to provide any information about the birds to you.

    Casually enquire about the diet, the grooming process, and other care requirements of the bird. Ask where the bird originates from and other questions about the species. If there is a lot of hesitation with respect to answering your queries, you need to understand that caretakers have no experience.

- **The birds are kept in poor conditions:** The conditions of the cage are very important for you to understand how they have been raised. A dingy and dirty cage is definitely a sign that the birds are not kept in the best conditions. However, in the case of pet stores, the bigger issue is that of overcrowding. Pet stores tend to just keep throwing new birds into the cages or aviaries. They take very little care about quarantining the birds as well.

    This means that birds are at the risk of infections, diseases and of course behavioral problems. Conures, in general, can dislike the idea of having to share their space with other birds. That means that they will retreat completely or will become extremely aggressive.

    Birds catch infections really easily. If the cage is already unkempt and the birds are crowded into these cages, you know that these birds may not be the best addition to your home unless you are able to take extra care of them.

4. Should you buy an adult or a baby?

This is a common dilemma faced by most people who want to bring home a pet bird. There are advantages and disadvantages of both and in this section we will discuss them in greater detail.

Bringing a baby conure home

A baby conure, like any other baby bird, is quicker to adapt to its new home. They will take a few hours to get used to the place that they have to live in for the rest of their lives

Usually, it is recommended that pet parents hand feed the babies. That way, you will be able to form a stronger bond with them. Baby conures will pick up behaviors that you teach them easily and it is also easier to correct any inherent behavioral problems like biting in the case of a baby bird.

You need to remember, however, that a baby bird is more delicate and you need to be extremely careful when it comes to handling them. They also need to be observed very closely for the first two days, especially if they have been newly weaned. You need to handle them for short periods of time regularly to get them used to you.

In addition to that, you also have to keep an eye on the feeding habits and droppings of the conure. If you notice any abnormality, it may be a warning sign for an impending health issue. At around 10 months of age, these birds molt and grown new plumes. That is a stressful period and can make them very nippy. Some conure owners will tell you that this stage is very hard to handle.

Bringing an adult conure home

You are most likely to bring home an adult from a rescue shelter. A conure that has passed puberty is called an adult. That is around the age of 2 for most of them.

When you bring home an adult conure that has been socialized or is used to handling, do not assume that you will have an easy task with the bird. Conures do get attached to their owners but may only get attached to one or two people at a time. The best thing about an adult is that you are aware of the personality. Depending on that, you may figure out how to get him to adapt.

29

Ehen you remove a conure from his environment, he will be under a lot of stress. This induces behavior like screaming and nipping. A bird that is stressed is also scared. That is why you may find it hard to handle him or her, but with some care and a reasonable adjustment period, you should be able to tame the adult conure. We will talk about this in greater detail in the next few chapters.

The benefits of bringing an adult home are that they are stronger than and not as delicate as the little ones. Once they have gotten used to your home, you may discover that they already know a couple of tricks that are interesting.

It does take some experience to care for an adult. If you are a first time parrot parent, you may want to think about bringing a baby home, as it is simpler.

5. Taking the bird home

Whether you look for a breeder, adopt a bird, or decide to buy one from a pet store, you need to take good care of how you make the transition to your home. You see, the journey to your home is quite a big deal for the conure and they tend to get very stressed.

As simple as this may sound, the drive home is a very important aspect of care. The movement and the several images that the bird will see as you drive past places can really confuse him. Like I said before, remember that we are dealing with a creature that is highly analytical and intelligent. This will cause a lot of stress. While that is unavoidable, you can make the experience a little more peaceful by following a few simple rules while driving your bird home from the breeder's or the pet store.

- Choose a smaller cage. Avoid boxes, as they will suffocate the bird and scare them. They will feel the movements but will not be able to see anything for themselves. This is not exactly a pleasurable experience. A very large cage means that there are chances of your bird having an accidental fall within the cage and injuring himself. He will probably be on the floor of the cage most of the time. When you are driving, the perch will feel unsteady. This is something that the birds absolutely hate. He will be uncomfortable and very scared. Let the bird be and just drive on.

30

- Keep water and food available. You can give the bird a bottle if he is already used to it. A water bowl needs to be monitored constantly. You do not want it splashing around. Chances are that the bird will be too stressed to eat or drink anything, however, it is good to have these basics available.

- Make sure that the car is not too hot or cold. Keeping your air conditioner on at room temperature is a must. The heat and cold will add to the bird's stress. In addition, keeping the windows down is not recommended. This will lead to drafts and strong winds that your bird will not appreciate.

- Do not talk to the bird. You may want to calm him down with comforting words, however, your voice is new to him and he will get stressed out with constant talking. If you are travelling with a friend or family member, do not talk much to them either. Music in the car is definitely not recommended. If possible, avoid busy roads.

When you reach home, just place the cage in the room reserved for the bird and leave him alone. Let him watch you and try to understand what is going on.

Chapter 3: When Your Conure Is Home

A large part of your relationship with your bird is dependent on the first few days of your bird being home. This is the time when you can actually make the bird feel comfortable and secure. The first day is especially crucial.

This chapter will tell you everything that you need to know about preparing your home for a green cheek conure.

1. Housing

The housing area should be arranged before you bring the bird home. That way, you can let the bird settle down as soon as he is home. Setting up after the bird is home would mean that he will have to make the transition from the carrier to his new home. This can be additionally stressful.

A nice cage makes a good enclosure for your green cheek conures and keeps them safe when you are away. Like we said before, the cage will become a nest for your birds, so make it as comfortable and beautiful as you can.

Size of the cage

With the cage, the bigger the better. However, there are some guidelines to follow for the minimum size of the housing space:

- The bird should be able to spread his wings in all directions.
- He should be able to jump from one perch to the next.
- He should be able to climb the bar with ease.
- He should be able to play with the toys in the cage.

For a small sized-bird like the green cheek conure, you need a cage that is at least 24"X24"30" in size. You need to ensure that the spacing of the bars is not more than 3/4th inch apart. This keeps them safe and prevents their feet or beaks from getting stuck.

What should it be made of?

When choosing a cage for your green cheek conure, there are two important requirements to keep in mind:

- The cage should be sturdy and it should have a very secure lock. Conures are highly intelligent and will learn to let themselves out if the lock is very easy. It is a good idea to get a padlock for the cage.
  The best material for the cage is either stainless steel or any other metal that is powder coated. Avoid buying circular cages or the cylindrical ones even though they look very ornamental and pretty.

  A rectangular or square cage is ideal for the birds to move around freely. Ideally, you should be able to access the food and water bowl from the door of the cage, or you will have to reach in every time you want to feed your bird. Some cages come with special openings that allow you to fill the food and water bowls quite easily.

- Make sure that you never buy cages made of iron, as it will rust. Of course, wood is not a good option, as green cheek conures are chewers. They will make their way out before you even know it.

  You need to get a guarantee that there are no traces of lead or zinc in the material used to construct the cage. This may lead to heavy metal poisoning, affecting the health of your conure.

Make the cage a haven for your bird, as he is likely to spend most of his time in it. There are several things that you need to add to the cage to make it fun and practical for the bird.

Ornaments and accessories

There are several ornaments and toys that you can choose from to make the cage a fun place for your green cheek conures to live in. You can place lots of perches made from different material and of varying thickness. If you have more than one bird in the cage, the perches should be large enough and strong enough to allow them all to perch simultaneously. That way you will not have to worry about overcrowding and related aggression.

Place food and water bowls in such a way that they are free from droppings. Most often, bird cages will come with assigned slots for these bowls. Make sure that all the birds, in the case of keeping multiple pets, have access to food and that there are enough food and water bowls for all of them.

You can have many toys for your green cheek conure. Like we discussed before, these birds need a lot of mental stimulation, which toys can provide. You will find toys that are designed specifically for birds. Make sure you pick only those to ensure the safety of your birds.

To make inexpensive toys for your bird, you can just roll some paper with treats and leave it in the cage. It will give your conure a fun foraging activity. Besides that, you can also use paper cut in different shapes to entertain your bird.

Substrate
Substrate refers to any material that you use to cover the bottom of your cage. These are usually absorbent material that can soak up any droppings. At the same time, they should be safe for the birds in case they are foraging on the floor of the cage. The best option is newspaper or plain paper. Never use the glossy newspaper inserts, as they may have some substances that are toxic for conures.

You must never use sawdust, corncob, wood chips or wood shavings that are generally recommended for poultry. These materials soak up the droppings and feces and will have mold growing all over them in no time. This can lead to infections in your conures.

It is a good idea to buy a cage with a grate just above the floor of the cage. This is good if you do not like the idea of your green cheek conures foraging through the messy substrate. If you do not have grates, pay special attention to the type of substrate you purchase.

Best food and water bowl options
The best choice for food and water dishes are steel cups. These do not scratch easily and are very easy to clean. It is important to ensure that the material is scratch proof as there can be a lot of bacterial growth in these spots, putting the birds at risk of infection. You can alternatively use ceramic bowls.

Water bottles are recommended by some green cheek conure owners as they prevent any droppings from getting into the food or water. The only problem with this is that it is hard to clean. In addition, the cap and seal may develop mold, too.

There are several readymade feeders and water dispensers that you can buy from a pet store. These may cost anything between $8-$20. If you don't mind shelling out this much money, it is a good idea to invest in these feeders, as they are usually designed to keep the food and water clean. Just make sure that the material that is used is safe for birds.

Cage placement

Birds are usually prey animals, so you need to place your cage or housing in a place where they feel safe. Do not put the cage where predatory animals are in the bird's sight. Of course, once you introduce our pets, this will not be of concern. In fact, your household pets are not a problem because you are always around. However, if the cage is placed near a window from which the neighbor's large St. Bernard is visible, take care.

Never place the cage on the floor or right in the middle of the room. This makes the green cheek conures feel vulnerable and may put them under a lot of stress. You do not want them to be placed in a room where there is a lot of noise from traffic, either.

The best option for a green cheek conure cage is against the wall in a position where the bird can get a full view of the room. If your conure is very timid, you may consider covering a portion of the cage with a blanket or cover to give them an area that they can retreat to when they feel threatened.

Now, what you place around the cage also affects the health of your bird. Make sure you never leave cleaning supplies around the cage. The cage must not be near a vent or any place where you expect drafts.

For more than one bird

If you want to introduce a new bird or keep multiple birds in one housing space, here are some tips that will help you:

- All birds must have free access to food and water to avoid fights.

- For birds like green cheek conures, each one requires at least 12 inches of perching space.

- Buy a cage that will allow all the birds to simultaneously spread their wings without running into ornaments or each other.

- If you notice any aggressive behavior, immediately separate the birds.

36

Cage safety

Making the cage fun is no doubt necessary. However, you need to remember that green cheek conures are small birds that are susceptible to accidents with the slightest negligence.

There are several precautions that you need to take in order to make the cage safe for your bird. Some of them are:

- Choose a rectangular cage as opposed to a round one. In the case of round cages, the birds do not have anywhere to hide or retreat into when they are scared. These cages will also affect the feathers of the bird, especially the ones on the tail.

- It is best that you choose a powder coated or stainless steel cage. Others that are made of wrought iron or with a painted surface can be dangerous as they may have deposits of zinc or lead.

- The bars should be parallel all over the cage. They must not converge anywhere.

- The distance between two bars must be appropriate. The width must be such that the bird is not able to fit his head through them and should not be so small that the toes get stuck.

- Make sure that the bars are made of a strong enough material to withstand a bite from your conure, who will use his beak to climb up and down.

- If you are using any towels or covering material on the cage, then you should make sure that there are no threads or holes in them. This may lead to strangulation or may have the bird's toenails or legs entangled, leading to fractures or injuries.

- The cage should not have any protrusions or sharp edges. If your bird scrapes his body on these protrusions, it can lead to severe injuries that may cause infections.

2. Bird proofing your home

Birds are extremely fragile creatures. They can get caught in tight spaces, have cuts or injuries from sharp objects, or may even get electrocuted if you do not take enough care.

Of course, as your bird is trained and used to being out of the cage, you may want to let him out more often. That will require you to bird proof the house completely. It is recommended that you do this before you actually bring the bird home.

Here are some tips on bird proofing your home:

- The house should be 100% smoke free. In fact, many people recommend that homes with people who smoke should not have birds, as they can develop several respiratory issues.

- Keep the cage away from hard floors or concrete. If you clip the wings of your birds, you have to make sure that the bird will not fall and injure itself.

- Ceiling fans and table fans should be switched off when the bird is out. This is true even when your bird's wings are clipped. Even with wing clipping, a portion of the bird's flying ability is retained. As a result, there are chances that the feathers or wings may get damaged.

- Get covers for all your stovetops or install a door in the kitchen. The kitchen should be a "no access" spot for birds because of the potential dangers in this area. Hot stoves, knives, fumes etc. can be extremely harmful to your birds.

- Cover up all the loose wires and threads. Conures, being the inquisitive creatures they are, will tug at this and may end up injuring or electrocuting themselves.

- Make sure that doors and windows are closed whenever the bird is out of the cage. In case you have any self-closing mechanism for your doors, have them removed and install strong stoppers. You do not want any flight-related mishaps due to slamming doors.

- Remove all plants that are harmful for birds. You can consult your vet or can check on the net to make sure that none of the plants that you have are hazardous to your pet.

3. Let the bird settle in

As excited as you may be to show off your new pet or even play with him the day he is home, it is best that you avoid this. For conures or any other birds, the first day in your home is their first day in a new environment. The bird is accustomed to the environment at the breeder's, the shelter, or the pet store. Your house needs some getting used to. This can be made much easier if you let the bird settle down at his own pace and learn about his new home.

The first thing that you need to do is transfer the bird from the travel cage to the bird's actual cage. Open the door of the enclosure and place the door of the travel cage in front of it. Open the travel cage and wait for the bird to walk in voluntarily. That may take a couple of minutes; be patient. Make sure you do not rush the bird and stress him out.

It is a really good idea to leave the bird alone with some food and water on the first day. They will not really like an unfamiliar voice. That said, it is a recommendation from many bird owners that you should spend time with the bird that you plan to buy while he is at the breeder's or the pet store. That makes the housebreaking process a lot easier.

If you have a bird that has been hand tamed, it is a lot easier to handle him eventually. However, on the first day, even a hand-tamed bird must not be meddled with. They need to recover from the traumatic experience of the drive and the whole shift to a new home.

When you are handling the food and the water bowls, make sure that you do not stand over the cage. You need to be at the eye level of the bird. That way, he will not look at you as a predator or as someone who is dominating him. You do not want to threaten your green cheek conure by towering over his cage. Once you have given him water and food, simply pretend like he does not exist and go about your routine. This is hard because you are obviously excited about having the new bird. However, avoid interaction at least on the first day.

A towel is really useful for a new bird. Put a towel on the back of the cage and let the bird hide behind it when he wants to. This is a popular technique that is used even for birds that have lived with a family for a long time. Our homes are filled with lights and sounds, be it from the television, mobile phones and other appliances. Conures need at least 10 hours of sleep. This towel will help them hide from all the noise and just relax. You can even buy readymade curtains or tents that you can install for the birds to sleep in or behind.

Try not to talk to the bird too much. You see, these creatures form very quick mental associations. When the bird is stressed and you are constantly talking to him, he will relate your voice to stress. That will make the whole process of training him and bonding with him challenging for you. You may walk past the cage a couple of times to make him familiar with your presence, but, other than that, avoid any form of interaction on the first day.

Ask the breeder or the pet store assistants to clip the flight feathers of your bird. Usually, this is already done, however it is always a good idea to check. You do not want to come home and have your bird flying all over the house while transferring him to his enclosure. There are chances that you leave the cage door open accidentally. After all, you are not used to having a bird at home. Remember, if you have other pets at home, it is even more important to keep your bird safe.

For the first few weeks, you can progressively increase the interactions with your bird. To begin with, place your hands on the sides of the cage and see how the bird reacts. He will nibble at your fingers, come close to your hand and just try to feel you out a little bit. Let him get used to you.

The key is to make sure that your bird is in a place where he is able to see your family and your activities. That way, he familiarizes himself with your family. As people pass by the cage, the bird will take note of them and observe them very carefully.

Now, talking to the bird can be tricky. Make sure that you keep your voice as low as possible. Say the same phrase again and again. Use something common like, "Hello", "Hi pretty bird" etc. This may also encourage your bird to mimic you. The reason you need to use the same phrase is that the bird does not really have a vocabulary yet. He will relate to the sounds that you make. The call must be familiar if you want the bird to relate to them and start responding to them.

You know that your bird is making progress of he walks towards the door of the cage when you arrive. That means that he is fond of you and is looking forward to the interaction with you. At all times, you need to bear in mind that you must only interact with the bird when you are at eye level. Let him feel like an equal to you. That is when he will start to get comfortable. It is best that these interactions are limited to one or two members of the family for the first few weeks.

Then, you may introduce the rest of your family to the bird, one by one. Let them start off with the hands on the sides of the cage as mentioned above. Green cheek conures will always bond with the whole family but will definitely pick favorites. These birds are really choosy whether it comes to food, toys, or even the members of the family. If you take it slow, your bird will make some progress.

Then, when you think it is safe, just reach into the cage and offer your finger for a step up. If your bird is hand-tamed, chances are that he will slowly perch on the finger. If not, you can follow the simple trust building tips that are mentioned in the following chapter.

Is your conure stressed?
For the first few days, the bird may not eat that well. This is not really an issue as long as you see that the bird is easing up and is progressing to better eating habits. However, in some cases, there may be something that you are doing unknowingly that is stressing the bird out very badly. You need to watch out for the following stress signs in your green cheek conure:

- Skin mutilation or tail plucking.
- Sudden changes in personality; from being extremely quiet to becoming unnaturally loud, or vice versa.
- Pacing up and down the cage. This may happen on the floor or on the perch.
- Pinning of the eyes.
- Keeping the tail feathers fanned at all times.
- Keeping the chest and head feathers raised all the time.
- Evident weight loss.

- Refusal to eat.
- Excessive urination.
- Too much water consumption.

If you see this behavior even up to the third day in your home, take the bird to an avian vet immediately. It may not just be stress, but signs of some other health issue.

How to build trust
Conures are highly intelligent creatures. You need to be aware of it at all times when you are interacting with your green cheek conures. It does not matter whether your conure is pleasant in his behavior or even aggressive; the first thing that you need to establish is that you are comfortable in the environment that he is in. That means you need to keep him in a room where he can see you walking around and just being yourself.

After two to three days, your bird should be settled in quite comfortably. That is when you can introduce treats to your bird. The best treat to start out with is some type of seed. You can try feeding it with your fingers, but if you see that he does not respond or is scared of your fingers, you can give it with a spoon or maybe on a stick. When the bird begins to relish the treat, he will take it from your fingers too. If he still doesn't take it from your hand, just take the seed and place it next to the bird. Then when he comes for the treat, praise him. Continue just this for about a week. When he is eating out of your hands comfortably, the next step is to let him out of the enclosure. It may take up to two weeks at the most to reach this stage.

Make sure that the wings of your birds are clipped before you let him out of the cage. If that is not what you want to do, you must establish a secure environment for the bird before you let him out. This is a checklist that you need to follow before you let out a bird without clipped wings at ANY time:

- All the windows must be closed with the blinds pulled down.
- There should be no hot stovetops.
- Close the lids of the toilets.
- Keep all the doors shut.
- There should be no new people the first time.

- You should definitely not have other pets around until they have had a chance to bond.
- The fans should all be off.

Allow him to explore the area around the cage. He may perch on the door or maybe on the cage itself. When he is settled somewhere comfortable, give him a treat. What you need to know about conures is that they may not really leave the cage and go too far, as they are inherently territorial. When you put a treat into the food bowl, they will go back into the enclosure easily. If he does fly far, you can still lure him with a trail of his favorite treat. This is the initial stage of building trust that you need to work on before you get him to perch on your finger or on your shoulder.

4. Introductions

Once your bird is settled in, which will probably be a week after coming to your home, you can begin to introduce him or her to other birds and to the pets in your household.

You need to be sure that the bird is ready for introductions. Some signs are:

- The bird is curious when someone approaches the cage and does not back away.
- The body language is relaxed and not alert at all times.
- The vocalization shows that the bird is happy and relaxed.

We will talk about vocalization and body language in the next section so that you have a better idea about what to look for.

Introducing green cheek conures to other pets
Introducing your conure to your other house pets such as a cat or a dog requires a lot of caution. Even if your dog or cat is extremely friendly and gentle, they are a potential threat to your bird. This is because, in the wild, birds are prey animals, while cats and dogs are predators. This is an instinctively ingrained message that we cannot erase despite the training and conditioning process. It does not mean that your conure and your pet will never get along, it only means that leaving them to interact without any supervision is dangerous.

43

First, place the cage of your bird in a room where your pets will most often hang around. Then, watch the reaction of your pet. If they are very curious or excited at the sight of the bird, it is not time to let the bird out yet. In this excitement, your pet may accidentally harm the bird. The pet may only be trying to figure out who this new entrant in your home is, but you must still remain vigilant.

All you need to do is leave the cage there as long as your pets lose interest in the bird. They should not react to the bird's presence in your home. In the meantime, if you see that your pet is trying to perch on the cage or climb on it, discourage the behavior immediately. A sharp "No!" from your end should do the trick. This will lead to submissive behavior from your conure when you do let him out of the cage eventually.

When your cat or dog loses interest in the cage being in the room, let the bird out. Of course, you must only do this after you have trained the bird to step up and then go back into his cage. If not, you may not be able to get your bird away if your cat or dog decides to chase it around. Let them be for a while and see how your pet reacts. If you hear the slightest growl or see any discomfort in the pet's body language, get the bird away immediately.

You can try this a few times. If you see any negative behavior of your pet towards the bird, it is best that you keep the bird in the cage whenever your pet is around. It is in the nature of some pets to dislike birds.

You also have a problem on your hands if your pet likes the bird. A dog will place a sloppy lick on the bird if he grows fond of him. A cat may do the same. Remember that the saliva of your cat or dog is toxic for the bird.

Although you must familiarize your pet with your new bird, it is a good idea to never leave them alone at home unsupervised. If you do this, the animals must be in an enclosure. Otherwise, you may come home to an unintentional but unpleasant scene.

Introducing green cheek conures to other birds
If you have other birds in your household, you need to pay more attention to quarantining the bird. Introductions should only be made once the bird has been properly quarantined. This will ensure that he

does not have any health issues that may spread to the rest of the flock.

What is quarantining?

Quarantining is an important process if you are bringing a new bird home to a family with multiple birds. The problem with introducing a new bird is the ease of being infected by or infecting the other birds in your flock. Even if you have had the parrot examined by an avian vet within the first 72 hours and s/he has confirmed that your bird is healthy, quarantining is absolutely necessary.

Some birds could just be carriers of diseases. This means that they do not have any symptoms of the actual medical condition, however the microbes responsible for these infections are using the bird's body as a host.

So, when you bring home a new bird, you need to keep him away from the other birds for at least 30 days. Place him in a separate cage. You must not place this cage in the same room as the rest of the birds. However, make sure that your birds can hear the new bird. That way, they know that someone new is in the family.

In this time frame, observe the new bird carefully. If he does not show any change in his behavior, routine, eating habits or even health, you can be sure that it is safe to introduce him to the rest of the flock.

However, even the slightest abnormality is a cause for concern. Take the bird to the vet immediately and have him checked for any possible infection. Then, when you are sure that the bird can be introduced to your flock, you can go ahead with the whole process. Yes, introducing birds is not as simple as putting the new bird in a cage or aviary with the rest of the birds. It is a lot of work and requires a good deal of patience.

The actual introduction

The introduction depends on whether the birds in your flock are from the same family or from different species. The wings of pet birds are usually clipped, so in the event of any confrontation between the birds, flying to safety is not an option. The birds therefore end up with no choice but to fight. It is for this reason that introducing your conure to other birds, especially ones larger than them, can be tricky. In fact, most conure or parrot injuries are related to other birds and not so much to pets like cats and dogs.

In addition to this, most birds, especially conures, tend to treat their cages as their nests and can get extremely protective or territorial about it. So if you think that it is safe to place your new bird in the same cage as the other, you need to think again. Sometimes, you may have no problem at all, but in other cases, you will discover that your birds just can't be the best of friends. There are some ways you can get your older birds to meet the new ones without creating much tension.

First, let us learn a little about bird psychology. Normally, birds like conures will not fight in the wild. They only bluff one another by keeping the posture erect. However, during mating season, they do get into physical fights, mostly attacking the feet, beaks, and eyes of one another. You may observe this sort of behavior only when one bird lands on the cage of the other. When you are introducing the birds to one another, the ground rule is "do not let them get on or in each other's cage".

So what should you do? Here are some tips to introduce your birds:

- Pay good attention to the birds in your house and note their reactions when you place their cages in the same room. Who is the most aggressive? Have any of your older birds displayed aggression towards other birds?

- Start with individual introductions. If you have just one more bird, you will have to stick to just these. When you have multiple birds, you will have to take it slow and move on to the group introduction phase. Make the space neutral. Give them perches that are on the same level so that they do not feel any threat. Choose the least aggressive bird and introduce him to your new conure. If they are quiet and not nippy, reward them and put them back to the cage. Introduce your onure individually to all your birds in this way. If you see that one of them is being too aggressive and may chase or bite your new conure, go back to the earlier steps and introduce them to each other in separate cages. You must do this until your conure is familiar with the individual birds. That may take about a week or two.

- The next step is to try a group introduction. Let them all out of their cages and make sure you close the doors of the cages. That way, no bird will get back in and there is no chance of fights because of perching. You need to be in the room when this happens and just let them settle for a few minutes. If you see any signs of aggression, direct the aggressive bird back to his cage with a treat. These group introductions may take varying amounts of time to become easy for the birds. You must always supervise these introductions. Sometimes, it may take even close to three months to be sure that the birds are not aggressive towards one another.

- If you have an aviary, you can put your new bird in the cage with the others after these group interactions. This also requires a lot of supervision because the cage is not a neutral space for your new bird as the others, particularly a few, will show dominance in their territory. Even this interaction can be varied and the time taken to adjust to one another in this non-neutral environment may extend to a few months.

- Once these interactions are calm, it is safe to introduce several perches and toys to the birds even in the presence of the new conure. In case you see that your conure is unable to get along with the old birds even after a period of three months, just allow him to have his own cage. This is especially true when you have birds that have formed a strong bond with one another or even if you have a single bird who has formed a strong bond with you.

No matter who you are introducing the bird to, whether it is another pet or another member of your family, make sure that you take it slow. Never rush the bird, as it may lead to stress. With birds, stress is one of the most common causes for severe health issues. This is because their immunity is compromised, making them vulnerable to diseases.

Chapter 4: Caring for Green Cheek Conures

Caring for your green cheek conure requires a good understanding of what your bird needs. Good care is the first step towards ensuring that your bird is healthy and happy.

1. What to feed green cheek conures?

Many first time owners are quite confused about what to feed their birds. There is a lot of contrasting information about what is good for your bird and what isn't, so it can be a little difficult. That said, there are a few things that are worth knowing about green cheek conures:

- They are not fussy eaters but they do pick their favorites.
- Overfeeding can make them gain weight.
- They need a lot of vitamins and calcium.
- The food consumed may increase during the breeding or mating season.

Getting the basics right

Conures eat a large variety of foods including seeds, nuts and fresh fruits and vegetables. Some conure owners also give their pets eggs in small portions. If your conure develops a liking for this, you can even leave a small amount of the shell on, as it is very good for the birds.

To begin with you need to find a certain measure of the food that you are giving your conure. It can take a while to get the exact amount and you may even have to do a few trials and errors to see how much your conure will eat in one sitting. It is a good idea to go by tablespoon measures.

The truth about pellets

The first thing that you need to give your conure is dry pellets. Choose natural pellets from brands like Zupreem or Harrisons. If you choose the former, it can make up for 30% of your bird's diet, but if you choose the latter, it should not be more than 10% of your bird's diet. The rest of it should contain fruits and veggies along with treats.

Avoid colored or dyed pellets, as they may harm the bird. Pellets are made from crushed seeds and are full of fiber. They include a lot of vitamins and minerals such as calcium along with fruits and vegetables. These are all essentials in your conure's diet. You can start the day out with these pellets and actually make them the staple of the diet. You can give a conure about 2 tablespoons of dry pellets a day.

Pellets are best stored frozen. Brands like Zupreem may spoil easily and need to be frozen. Pellets contain several nutrients and are hence a lot better for your bird than an all seed diet, as only seeds can cause health issues in the bird. Give your conure fresh pellets every morning. Remove the left overs and refill the food bowl every day.

Adding seed treats in between the pellets is a great idea and necessary for your bird's diet. You get seed treats like nutriberries that will add a lot of minerals and vitamins to the conure's diet. Ideally, birds as small as the green cheek conure will consume about 2 to 4 of these in a day. You can give them in between meals, ideally when they are half done with the pellets and once the pellets are fully done. There are other such treats as well that birds may like and you should be able to find them in any store.

Fruits and Vegetables
These are crucial parts of a bird's diet. Although some avian vets will tell you otherwise, many conure owners will tell you from their personal experience that these birds need fruits and vegetables in order to stay as healthy as possible. Even in the wild, birds eat fruits and vegetables.

You should ideally give a green cheek conure 1 tablespoon of vegetables and 1 tablespoon of fruits a day. If you think that they will eat more, you must increase the vegetable portion. Vegetables give the birds a larger amount of vitamin A, which is essential for them. Fruits give them the vitamins that they need but also act as flavor addition to the bird's food.

In order to offer the fruits or vegetables, you can mix two or more varieties of each and heat them a little in the microwave, just to make them warm. Then, you may mash them and feed them to your bird. Now, sometimes birds may not develop any taste for these fruits and vegetables, so you can add stronger flavors like strawberry or blueberry juice. These are great foods to include but always remember that the portion of vegetables must be higher than the fruit. Here are some good fruit and vegetable options for your birds:

Grapes
Apples
Pomegranate
Melon
Mango
Pineapple
Papaya
Kiwi
Watermelon
Star fruit
Blueberries
Cherries
Blackberries
Broccoli
Carrots
Beans
Sweetcorn
Peppers
Spinach
Sweet potato
Butternut Squash
Red Cabbage
Beetroot
Sprouts

You can divide the 1-tablespoon portion across the day and feed them to your bird. You must offer this separately from the pellets and you will notice that your bird will pick his favorites. Offering seasonal fruits and vegetables can be great for your bird but before you introduce any new food to the conure, ask a vet or do enough research to be sure that it is safe.

What not to feed your birds:

- **Peanuts:** While other nuts like hazelnuts can be great for the conure, as they are a source of protein, peanuts can cause health problems because of fungal toxins.

- **Onions and Garlic:** These two should not be offered in any form to the conures, as they cause some irritation to begin with. In addition to that, they can make your conure very anemic.

- **Tomatoes:** Tomatoes, especially raw ones, are hazardous to birds as they are acidic vegetables. They potentially cause ulcers in green cheek conures.

- **Mushrooms:** They can cause serious digestive issues and even liver failure in green cheek conures.

- **Celery:** If you can remove all the stringy part of celery, it is quite safe to feed to your conure. If not, it may lead to crop impactation.

- **Avocados:** Avocadoes are poisonous for conures. They contain a certain toxin called perrsin that can cause breathing difficulties or even kill your conure.

When you are uncertain of a certain food, be sure that you consult your vet or fellow conure owners. When you are sure that it is of no harm to your bird, you can introduce the birds to it.

What if the bird dislikes pellets?

This is a common problem faced by conure owners. Usually our birds come home from a pet store or from breeders. If they have been accustomed to a seed diet, they may not take an instant liking to pellets. Most conures who are on a mainly seed diet will experience some health issues, the most pressing one being obesity.

One great way to introduce your bird to pellets is to include a small amount in the current seed diet, and then when he begins to eat that small amount, you may increase it. Keep increasing the proportion of the pellets until the seeds are completely out of the diet.

Another way to go about this is to give your conure mashed pellets. You can soak pellets in warm water until they are soft enough to crush. You can offer this to the bird and see if he or she eats it. If not, you can add a small amount of flavor inducer such as agave syrup, cranberry juice or even sunflower kernels to the crushed pellets. Make sure that you just add a tiny pinch of flavor that is enough to attract the bird but not so much that it makes your conure addicted to that flavor.

Whenever you are making a change to your conure's diet, consult your vet. It is important to make sure that this diet change is not causing weight loss in your bird. You can monitor this at home on a scale or you have to work with an avian vet.

Sunflower seeds can be beneficial to your bird in very small amounts, maybe once a week. They do cause rapid weight gain but when given sparingly can be a great source of protein and Vitamin E.

The feeding routine
The final question is how often should you feed your conure? Ideally, feeding the bird twice a day with a few treats in between can work really well. In the morning, offer the pellets first. Then at about 11 am, you can give the bird one serving of a vegetable. Then in the evening at about 4 pm, you can give him the portion of fruit. In between these meals you may offer seed treats like nurtiberries. Establish a routine with your conure to ensure that he is eating on time.

Measure the amount of food per meal to make sure that your bird does not overeat. You will know that your bird is done eating at a given meal time when he shows loss of interest in the food. Offer him only this much per sitting to avoid overeating. Only the pellets can be made available all day. That should also be done in controlled proportions of 2 tablespoons a day. Replace the water in the dish regularly, as conures may dip their food in the water and dirty it.

2. Keeping the cage clean
It is mandatory that you have a daily cleaning routine for the main parts of the cage every single day. If you are not willing to do this, you must not commit to having a bird. Here are some simple

practices that will make sure that your bird has a healthy and sanitary environment.

The right cleaning material
The cleaning material that you choose should be safe for the bird and must be able to thoroughly disinfect the cage. A bird's cage is full of pathogens that you need to clean up fully.

You may use soap and water if there is any organic material or debris that you want to remove. The solution must be very mild to prevent any irritation. Remember that soap and water does not disinfect the cage. You need to wipe the cage down with a disinfectant to make sure that it is actually free from germs and microbes.

Bleaching powder is one of the best and most easily available disinfectants. You can make a dilute solution and wipe all the contents of the cage down. Make sure that your bird is out of the cage when you do this, as the fumes can irritate the bird. You can put him back after the solution has dried completely and the distinct smell is gone. If the cage is made of metal, bleaching powder may reduce its usage time.

An alternative is Nolvasan, which is readily available in any pet store. You could also use Virosan, as it is safe for your bird. Although these products are expensive, they are very useful for the cleanliness of your bird's cage. Most of the pathogens will be eliminated with these products.

Stabilized chlorine dioxide is also a good choice to disinfect the cage. The advantage with this product is that it uses oxidation to disinfect. That makes it effective even against spores and viruses. This product is also very safe. It is used to clean drinking water in many parts of Europe. There are no side effects or damages caused by the use of this product. It is also safe to clean the feeders and the water bowls with this product. You just have to spray it on the surface that you want to clean and wipe it down. And, voila! Your bird's cage is free from any threats.

The cleaning schedule
Three are some things that you have to do on a daily basis to ensure the overall cleanliness of the cage. You can clean the cage

thoroughly on a weekly or fortnightly basis. Here is a schedule that you can maintain for cage cleaning.

Daily cleaning

The food and water containers must be cleaned on a daily basis. If you use steel or porcelain ones, they are easiest to clean. It is a good idea to keep a spare pair that you can use when the ones that you have washed are drying. Use a cleansing gel that you can get in a pet store to clean the bowl. Then, rinse it with water. Never leave any chemical behind, as it may seriously harm your bird. These bowls need to be fully dry before they are replaced.

The substrate needs to be removed and replaced on a daily basis. Most of the moisture is retained in the substrate and should be removed to prevent any fungal or bacterial growth.

Any surface that is exposed must be wiped down on a daily basis. You can use one of the disinfectants mentioned above in a very dilute form, spray it on the surface and then wipe it down after leaving it on for about 1 hour. This is one way to make sure that your cage is sanitized and clean. In addition to that, it also increases the life of the cage.

Weekly or fortnightly cleaning

It is a good idea to remove all the toys from the cage every fortnight and clean them thoroughly. Any severely damaged ones can be thrown away. Use a brush to remove any dry organic matter. If you notice that one of the toys is very dirty, wash it immediately and dry it before replacing it. Soak the toys in a cleansing solution and rinse them completely. No chemical from the cleaning agent should be left behind, as it is harmful for your bird. Then, make sure that they are fully dry before you put them back in the cage.

Make it a monthly practice to wash the cage out thoroughly. You will have to use a brush to scrub out any dry material from the floor or the cage. Using warm water makes it easier to clean the dirty parts of the cage. You can simply use a soap water solution. Then, wash and rinse the cage fully. Once it is dry, spray a disinfectant and wash it down. Of course, you will have to have a standby enclosure for your bird. Do not put the bird back until the cage is fully dry.

Some of you may want to keep the cage outdoors. In this case, you must wash the whole cage twice a month. That will make sure that any pathogens that have been released into the cage by wild birds or rodents will be removed. It will also keep dust at bay.

If your bird has not been hand trained, you will need to use a towel to handle the bird. Wrap the towel around his body. Allow the ends to fall over your hands and protect them from any bites. Make sure that the head is not covered by the cloth. You can also use sturdy gloves to protect yourself from accidents.

The cage that you transfer your bird to must have a lot of food and water if this is the first time. Once the bird is trained and accustomed to this routine, it will be a lot easier for you. In case you are unsure of what cleansing agent you can use, consult your vet first. It is recommended that you check the cage thoroughly every day. In case you find any debris or peculiar droppings, clean it instantly. You definitely do not want to leave pieces of rotting food around. With all species of parrots, you will also have to clean out the things that they hoard in their cage as part of their nesting habits.

3. Grooming your conure

Grooming is not just important to keep the bird clean; it is also a very important part of bonding with your bird. In the wild, conures groom one another to show affection. You can maintain a regular grooming routine with your bird, too.

This will also help you discover any abnormalities on the bird's body or in the plumage. This could be a sign of underlying health issues. Grooming helps you detect them early so that your bird can get immediate medical attention.

Bathing your green cheek conure

In general, conures like to stay clean. They have several instinctive cleaning methods in the wild. You need to be able to provide the one factor that the birds miss, which is rain, through a regular bath. As you know, green cheek conures are from tropical parts of the world where rainfall is common, so it is essential for them to stay clean. Besides that, they have three natural ways of keeping their bodies free from any dirt:

Powdering down: This refers to a small amount of dander or powder that the birds produce from the feathers. All conures have down feathers that continue to grow for long periods of time. These feathers have very fine extensions that break often. This powder coats the feathers and the body of the bird. This powder repels water and dirt. It sticks to the dirt and when the bird preens itself, falls down with the dirt. The more dander the bird produces, the healthier he will be. Of course, this is not a welcome instinct for most pet conures.

Preening: This is the healthiest natural grooming method for the birds. It is useful to scape feathers and keep them moist. You will see your green cheek conure use the water from the bowls to preen himself. Besides that, preening ensures that all the feathers of the bird are in place and can be used properly. In the wild, parrots of any kind will not let one feather go out of place because it makes them more vulnerable to predator attacks. A feather sticking out means that the predator will be able to spot the bird in a flock.

When they preen themselves, these birds also break a certain gland known as the Preen Gland or the Uropygial Gland that is present just at the base of the tail. This gland produces a certain oil that the birds rub all over their feathers just to make them water proof.

How to bathe your conure

If this is the first time your conure is taking a bath in your home, you need to make it a pleasant memory for him. Sometimes, when they have been bathed very harshly in their younger days at the breeders' or at the pet store they will develop a negative feeling towards bathing. They may scream and rant when they hear the sound of a water tub filling up.

In order to give your conure a bath, just fill up a small birdbath or even sink with water and lead the bird to it. You can use toys or treats to do this. Allow them to stand at the edge of the sink and just explore. They may be excited but scared to get into the water.

In order to lower the conure into the tub, allow them to perch on your palm and slowly lower him towards the water, then let the bird step in. In about ten seconds of entering the water tub, the bird should become familiar with or just used to it. Keep talking to your bird and make him feel safe. Praise him when he is wading in the water. You can also put some of his favorite toys into the water.

If you need to use soap, it is safe to use any mild human soap or shampoo. However, it is recommended that you buy specially made soaps to avoid any sort of allergy or infection. You can make a diluted soap solution and use your hands to create a lather. Take a lot of care to avoid getting any in his eyes. In case of thick dirt, you can use a washcloth or a very soft tooth brush to gently brush it off. Then rinse the bird well with clean, warm water and use a towel to pat him dry.

Some conure owners use hair dryers to dry their birds, but it is recommended that you let the bird dry naturally as this gives them a chance to even preen their feathers into place. Of course you need to make sure that the air-conditioning and the fans are off in the room where the bird is drying himself off.

For fully-grown conures, a bath is not necessary. You can simply spray some water on them or just allow them to walk around under the shower. You will get special shower perches in any pet store that allow you to place the perch on the tiles of the shower wall with suction cups. Avoid using soaps during showers, as your bird may not allow you to get it all off. They will only stay under the shower for a few minutes and fly off. This is just to make up for their instinctive love of rain.

You can give your bird a thorough bath every fortnight. A light shower is recommended twice a week to keep the bird healthy and free from any infections. When you are putting them in a birdbath, make sure that it is very shallow, as parrots are not good swimmers as a general rule. It should just be enough for the bird to soak himself.

Nail and beak trimming
This grooming process is optional. If you notice that your bird's toes and beak are getting stuck in the toys or any fabric, you can trim it to avoid any accidents. If the beak or toe of your bird is stuck to the fabric on your upholstery and he tries to move suddenly, there are chances that the whole toe is ripped off or the beak is severely damaged. To avoid this, trim the sharp ends.

Wrap the bird with a towel, only exposing the part that you want to trim. In the case of the beak, gently lift the upper mandible with your finger and feel the sharp end. Keep the beak supported and trim the beak using a nail file. When you feel that it is just blunt, stop trimming. If the nail or toe is too short, the bird will be unable to climb and hold properly.

Even with the toe, make sure that you have a finger supporting the nail you want to trim to avoid any chances of breakage or unwanted damage.

It is a good idea to give your bird perches and toys of different textures. That will let the nails and the beak stay blunt naturally. As the bird climbs or chews with the proper toys, the beak and nails get trimmed. You will see them rubbing their beak onto rough surfaces as an attempt to keep them trimmed. This is an instinctive practice that should be encouraged.

Remember that bonding with birds as intelligent as conures requires a lot of effort from your end. These birds will analyze every situation that they are put into and even the slightest doubt will break their trust. If you have adopted a bird that has been abused, this will take longer. You will also need a lot of assistance from your avian vet to gain the trust of such birds. Take it one step at a time and make sure that you do not rush him.

Wing clipping
Some people believe that wing clipping is not ethically correct. If you are one of them, make sure that your home is a safe haven for your bird. You do not want to have any flight-related accidents at home. This may also lead to the escape and loss of your precious conure.

If you have pets at home, do not clip the wings. This is your bird's only form of defense. Even when you have multiple birds in an aviary, the wings should be intact to help your bird escape an aggressive cage mate.

If you decide to clip your bird's wings, make sure you have it done at the vet's the first time. You can learn how to do it, practice with your vet and then do it at home. You need to be very experienced to ensure that you do not accidentally get any blood feathers.

A bird must be hand tamed before you decide to clip his wings yourself. He must be comfortable enough to let you handle him. The first thing is to get your bird into a comfortable position to clip his wings. Pick him up using a towel and place him face down on your thigh. Then let the first wing out of the loose end of the towel and spread the feathers. Cut the primary feathers only. These are the largest feathers. The first three feathers are usually cut. You can snip about 1cm from each feather.

Then, repeat on the other side. Compare the wings to make sure that they are equal. If they are not, your bird will have difficulty walking or even perching. In case you do get a blood feather, make sure you apply styptic power to the wound immediately. If the bleeding does not stop, take the pet to the vet to have the shaft removed.

Clipping the wings only reduces your bird's ability to fly, it does not prevent flight altogether. So, when you take your bird outdoors, be vigilant. Even the slightest breeze can give him the lift he needs and lead to an escape. You need to clip the wings every 6 months.

4. What to do if the bird escapes

Even with clipped wings, the outdoors can be a challenge with your green cheeked conures. There could also be instances when the cage door is not secure and your bird gets out. A slight breeze is good enough to give the bird the lift that he needs to fly. If this happens, finding your bird can be hard. This is especially difficult for a bird as small as the green cheek conure.

There are a few things that you can do in order to look for your bird in case of an escape. This will increase your chances of finding your bird.

When you see your conure flying away

- Call out your bird's name loudly as he begins to fly. Birds are great at tracking sounds and are likely to get back to you when they hear you.

- Do not look away from your bird and keep your eyes on him for as long as you can. You will be able to tell how far he was able to get, the direction he went in and the possible area that he landed in if you do this.

- Call your friends and family immediately and try to get them to the spot it. The more people you have searching for the bird, the easier he will be to find.

Looking for the bird

- Once your friends and family have arrived, look around in the area that you saw the bird last in. You can cover a bigger radius if you have more people looking for the bird.

- There could be several phrases or sounds that your bird is familiar with. Shout them out along with the name of the bird as you are calling out to him. A lost bird will most likely call back when he hears you. He is definitely afraid and is trying to relocate his flock.

- If you have any recording of your parrot screaming on your phone, play it out. He may respond to this too.

- If your conure has a mate or a cage mate that he is closely bonded to, take the bird along in a cage and place him in the area that you last saw your bird. Stay away from this cage and wait. If the bird in the cage screams or shouts because you are away, the lost bird may respond.

- If you do not find the bird in this area, increase your search radius by 1 mile. It is very unlikely that your bird would have gone too far away. Only when the wind is too strong or if the bird has been chased by a predator will he get too far from home.

- In many cases, your bird may see you and become absolutely quiet. This is because he feels scared in your presence. So don't just rely on sound or a call back and keep searching for the bird with your eyes.

- Look for movement rather than color. Even with the bright plumes of the green cheek conure, you just may not be able to see him on a tree or behind bushes. Remember, he is green for the most part and that serves as a great camouflage.

When you find the bird

If you are lucky to find the bird but are unable to reach out to him, there are a couple of things that you can do to get him to come to you:

- The first thing to do would be to relax when you find the bird. If you get overly excited and jumpy, the bird may just fly away. Unless there is any danger around him, just let the bird stay where he is.

- The human that the bird is closest to is the best person to call out to him. You can even bring the bird's cage mate to lure him down.

- Hold out the foods that your bird likes to eat. You can even keep the bird's favorite toy and his food and water bowls out. When he sees something familiar, it is likely that he will fly to it.

- If your bird's wings are clipped, do not urge him to fly down from a very high branch. While he may have gone up there because of the wind, he may not be able to come back down just as easily. You may have to get up to the bird and hold the cage or perch out to a place where he will have to take a short flight to reach it.

- Do not raise anything unfamiliar towards the bird. He will definitely back away and get further away from you. He is probably very scared already and will not appreciate anything alien coming towards him. If the bird assumes a flight position, stop whatever you are doing.

- Hide from your bird. When he sees that you are gone, he will scream and call out and will try to approach you the moment he sees you again. You will notice the anxiety in your bird as he will start to flutter his wings and will also call out to you. The moment you notice this, let him see you.

- Do not crowd around the bird's favorite member of the family. Even if he wants to fly down, he may avoid it because he is too scared.

If the bird is out after sunset

If you cannot reach for the bird, let him sleep. You must look around for owls. If there are any traces, they may chase your bird away and you have to either stay put or look for ways to get the bird down. If you are certain that there are no owls, let your bird rest and you can come back for him in the morning, as he is likely to stay in the same place.

If the bird is missing for a whole day

If you have not managed to spot your bird for 24 hours or more, you may have to seek professional assistance to get your bird. There are a few organizations that you can call for help including:

- The local animal control.
- SPCA or the humane society.
- Your vet.
- Local zoos.
- Pet shops around your area.
- The local police.
- You may place an advertisement in the classifieds section of papers.
- You must also constantly check the found section of classifieds to see if anyone has found your bird.
- Post several flyers of the lost bird around the neighborhood.

Never give up hope of getting your bird back. Keep looking for him. Chances are they may even find their way back home before you know   it.

Chapter 5: Bonding With Your Green Cheek Conure

Like any other bird from the parrot species, green cheek conures tend to form strong bonds. The bond that your bird forms with you depends entirely on the effort that you put in during the initial days of your bird coming into your home.

Conures are playful birds and love to spend time outside the cage. This is something that you can enjoy with your bird too. However, you need to make sure that you understand your bird properly and that you train him well.

Good training makes it possible for your bird to socialize a lot better. It will also keep the bird safe when he is let out of the cage.

1. Understanding the language of your bird

Birds do communicate with us. It is up to the owners to spend time understanding the bird and learning the language of the birds. Birds use two methods to communicate - vocalization and body language. This is quite consistent and with regular interaction with your bird you will be able to understand what your bird is trying to communicate to you.

Understanding vocalization or sounds

Green cheek conures can be extremely vocal birds. In fact, they have the reputation of being too noisy and talkative. This is quite a good thing, however, because your bird will constantly communicate with you. There are some noises and sounds that your bird will make. Becoming familiar with this will help you understand what to expect.

- **Talking, whistling and singing:** This means that your bird is happy and content.

- **Chattering:** The most commonly used method to get your attention. This is seen in birds that are still learning to talk.

- **Clicking the tongue:** They are just having fun or are asking you to do something fun with them.

63

- **Low growl:** This is a sign of aggression and shows that something is troubling or threatening the conure. Look for objects that your bird dislikes and get it out of their sight. Never handle a growling conure.

Understanding the body language of conures

Most of the communication takes place through the body language of the bird. Watching the way the bird stands, moves, and uses his wings or beak will tell you a lot about what he is thinking and feeling. Here are some typical conure gestures and postures that you should keep an eye out for:

- **Flashing the pupils**: All parrots can control their pupils. If they dilate them, it is an indication of pleasure, anger or nervousness. You need to examine the surroundings of the bird to understand what this "pinning" or "flashing" signifies.

- **Tongue clicking**: This is a sign of pleasure and is often an invitation to you to come and play with him.

- **Beak clicking**: A sharp clicking sound made from the beak shows that your bird is feeling threatened. There could be some object or person in the room that the bird is scared of. He will additionally raise a foot and also extend his neck almost as if he is defending the cage.

- **Beak grinding:** You will hear the bird grinding his beak at night mostly. This is a sign of satisfaction and security.

- **Beak wiping**: When the bird is in an aviary, this is a sign of defense against the other birds or a warning sign. If your bird is alone and displaying this behavior, he is trying to get something out of his beak.

- **Regurgitation**: This behavior is displayed to their mates. Usually, a bird will regurgitate food and feed the contents to its partner. This is what he is trying to do if he has a strong bond with you.

- **Head snaking**: If your bird moves the head from side to side almost like he is dancing or waving the head, he is trying to get your attention. The bird will even tilt his head to one side and look at you as a sign of interest in what you are doing.

- **Lowering the head**: The bird will pull his wings close and lower the head and will almost look like he is about to fly. This is his way of telling you that he wants to come to you.

- **Beak fencing:** This is only seen when there are multiple birds in the cage. The birds will hold each other's beak almost like they are jousting. It is considered to be some sort of sexual behavior.

- **Panting:** If your bird is overheated or is too exhausted, then panting is observed. It is basically a sign of discomfort.

- **Wing drooping:** This is normal in young birds. If your bird is an adult, then it is a sign of illness.

- **Wing flipping:** A sharp flip or flick of the wing shows displeasure. It could also mean that your bird is just trying to set his feathers in place.

- **Quivering:** If the body or wings quiver, it is a sign of distrust. Talk to such a bird in a calm and comforting voice.

- **Marching:** If the bird marches with his head down, he is being defensive or aggressive. On the other hand, if his head is up, he is inviting you to play with him.

- **Tail bobbing:** This is usually a sign of sickness or fatigue, especially when the tail bobs when your bird is breathing.

- **Tail wagging:** When the bird sees his favorite person or toy, he wags his tail as a sign of happiness.

- **Tail fanning:** This is a dominant or aggressive behavior that basically tells you to back off.

- **Barking:** The bird is not mimicking another pet in your home. This is a natural vocalization that that is meant to show dominance.

- **Purring:** If the bird's body is relaxed when he is purring, it shows contentment. However, if the body is still and the pupils are dilated, it is a sign of aggression.

Learning these simple postures and vocalizations of the birds can help train the birds better, too. You will also enjoy playing with your bird a lot more when you are familiar with his language. It is a great insight into the personality of your bird.

2. Training your conure

Green cheek conures are extremely intelligent birds. Training them is a major part of bonding with them. You can teach them simple and advanced tricks quite easily. Training is also a great mental activity for your bird.

With a bird like the green cheek conure, mental stimulation is extremely important in keeping the bird healthy and free from any bad behavior. A bored conure can be a nightmare, as they develop issues like feather plucking or screaming.

a) Basic training

Basic training includes a few commands that your bird should be able to understand. These commands are extremely necessary when your bird is let out of the cage. They ensure that your bird is safe and that you are able to handle your bird easily when he is outside.

Step up training

Step up training is the best display of trust towards the owner. Not only does the step up training form the basis of building the relationship, it is also one of the most important things to teach your green cheek conure. In the case of an emergency such as a fire or a natural disaster, you should be able to reach in and have the bird step up on your finger in order to escape. If you do not train the bird to step up, he may not let you handle him and pet him either. That makes it very difficult to do the other fun things like teaching him tricks and generally including him in various activities throughout your day.

Here are a few tips to train your bird to step up:

- Your hands are very scary for a new green cheek conure and don't forget, their cage is their home. When you just intrude and put your hands through, you are most likely to get bitten. So take it as slow as you possibly can.

- You will need a lot of treats that you can feed them with your hands if they are comfortable or with a spoon or a stick. When you have successfully taught your conure to come out of the cage, you are ready to have them step up on your finger.

- The first thing to do would be to lead the bird to the open door of the cage. Then, you can offer your finger like a perch just a few centimeters away from the door.

- Remember to hold the finger horizontally so that it looks like a branch and do not point at the bird in such a way that your fingers look like food to them.

- Then, hold the treat behind the perch finger.

- At this point, they may immediately step up or may hesitate. Do not
stress them too much.

- Offer the step up command about two to three times and if the bird only looks at the treat and does not come for it, put the treat back in the food bowl and try again.

- It is also possible that your bird will put his beak around your perch finger and gently nibble. They are not biting and you must never draw your hand back. In the wild, birds do this to make sure that the perch is steady. So, if your bird bites your finger and you hold it still, he will probably step up, but if you draw the finger away, he will lose trust in your finger.

- When he climbs up, offer him a treat. Let him stay for a while and put him back in the cage.

- Offer him a final treat before closing the cage door.

- Keep doing this for a few days. Place your perch finger, say "step up" and when he does, offer a treat. Soon, just the step up command without the treat is good enough. Remember to praise your bird abundantly irrespective of whether he makes progress or not.

- After you have taught the bird to step up on your finger, you can offer your shoulder as the next step.

- You will do the same thing, hold the bird up to your shoulder and when he steps on to it, offer him a treat. That way you can lead him up to your head as well.

- Getting the bird on your shoulder is great progress, as it allows you to include him in all your daily activities. You can keep him on your shoulder as you fold laundry, do the dishes or even just sit down and read a book. That way, he will feel like you are giving him attention and is likely to bond faster.

Once you have established the trust to get the conure to step up on to your finger, you can try to pet him. Start by stroking the head and the cheeks. If he allows you to do that, you can move on to the critical part which is touching the beak. If your conure allows you to touch the beak without biting, then it means that he has established a high level of trust in you.

Teaching your conure not to bite

There are two reasons why your green cheek conure may bite - defense and attention. However, biting of any kind must be discouraged. The bird must know that it is not acceptable behavior. If you are able to build trust with the conure, biting will significantly stop. There are other things that you can try to reduce to stop your bird from biting.

In the initial days of your interaction with your conure, biting only comes from fear, so you need to be patient. If your bird bites you when you are trying to get them to perch on your finger, you have to remember not to shout or scream.

The moment you do that, the bird gets a message that this is how they can control you and stop you from doing what they are not fond of. Instead, you just let the bird back in the cage and try again.

The next thing is when your conure has started perching on your hand but begins to bite when you are trying to pet it. That is when you have a little more trust with the bird. You can gently push the head down with your index finger. It is a small and slight push that should not hurt the bird. Then in a very soft voice say "no biting". Attempt to pet the conure again until you have a positive reaction.

Just stroking the cheek is good. When this happens, praise the bird for being good, put the bird back in the cage and give him a closing treat. At this stage, the bird finds the cage to be a positive reinforcement.

The last type of biting that you want to discourage is "demand" bites. This is when you have established a good relationship with your bird and he nips at you when he wants something that is in your hand. For instance, if he is on your shoulder and you have a fruit in your hand, he will bite your ear or cheek. There are two things that you can do.

First, you can just return the bird to the cage. This stops the behavior, as the bird wants to be with you at this stage and going back to the cage is not as much fun as being with you.

The next thing is to shake his balance. If he is on your head or shoulder, you can actually run or jog. That puts the bird off balance and will make him release the beak. If he is on your finger, you can gently shake your hand or simply raise your elbow. Losing balance is something that conures hate and they will stop any behavior that leads to it.

Stopping your conure from screaming

As mentioned before, conures can be extremely noisy. They can even begin to scream to seek attention or to make you do something they want you to. Both of these are not good and must be curbed.

There are certain times of the day when the bird calls out instinctively. This is usually at dawn or dusk. Although this can be loud and extremely noisy, it is instinctive behavior. You must be sure that you can deal with some noise during the day. In addition, make sure your neighbors do not complain.

The only time the screaming becomes a problem is when your conure begins to scream every time you leave the room. That means he is only screaming for your attention and nothing more. So, here are a couple of things that you do not want to do when you observe this behavior:

- Do not scream back at the bird and instead say, "stop" or "don't scream".

- Do not come running back into the room every time to just get him to stop screaming. This encourages screaming. When you respond with your own voice or by coming to the bird, you are doing exactly what they want. You are their "Ffock" that is calling back when they call, so they are happy to have your attention and will continue to scream.

- Unlike dogs or cats, a sharp "no!" is actually not a negative thing for birds. They think of it as your call in response to theirs.

- Instead, it is a good idea to put some toy or treat in the cage before you leave the room. That way they have something more interesting and something to distract them. It tells them that you going away means that it is time for some fun inside the cage.

- The next thing you can do is just let the bird scream and not come back. Wait for the screaming to stop and then go in and reward your bird. That way, the bird understands that you will come back when he is quiet and will also reward him. Eventually, the period of silence will increase.

- Some people will tell you to put a blanket on the cage when the bird screams. While this works, it is negative reinforcement. Hence, it is discouraged.

b) Advanced training

Do not move on to these commands and tricks unless your bird has mastered the ones mentioned above. This can be extremely confusing for the bird and can make the task a lot harder on your part.

Potty training

Surprisingly, it is possible for you to potty train a green cheek conure. It just requires you to understand the pooping cycle and body language of your bird.

A small bird like a green cheek conure will poop every 10 to 15 minutes and if you want to avoid accidents when your bird is out of the cage, you need to potty train him. Here are some simple tricks to teach your bird to poop where you want them to:

- The first thing to do would be to teach him to poop inside the cage in the morning.

- Before feeding, put a paper on the floor of the cage and wait for the bird to poop.

- They will show a very distinct type of body language, which is usually lifting their tail and leaning down on the perch. Then, when they do poop, praise them abundantly and offer a treat that is part of the diet.

- The next step is to watch for these signs after you have taught your bird to step up.

- When you see the pooping body language, hold them over a trashcan or over a piece of paper. Then when they do poop on that, they need to be praised abundantly. That way, they know that there is one place or appropriate place for them to poop and they will not mess the whole house up.

71

Teaching conures to talk

Unlike other species of parrots like the Eclectus parrot, green cheek conures are not the best at learning to talk. They are intelligent enough to pick up a few words and it is fun to teach them a few as well.

Typically, they may learn up to 10 words in their lifetime, so you need to choose what you want to teach them. Green cheek conures don't really learn the meaning of words but only learn to mimic you. They will associate it with a particular action if you say the word before that action like a command. Here are a few tips to teach your conure new words:

- Pick a word that you want to teach him. Suppose you pick, "hello", you need to say this everyday at a specific time.

- Make sure there are no distractions like TV sounds when you are saying the word that you want to teach him.

- Now associate that with an action that he will remember like you walking into a room.

- Say it in a high-pitched voice and sound as excited as you can.

- If you are really excited, he will feel motivated to learn that call, as it is positive to him.

- Eventually, when you enter the room, he will respond with a high pitched, "hello". Be patient.

Teaching conures to lay on their back

This is a really cute trick to teach your conure. They are very happy to lay on their backs and are among the few birds that can actually do this. Initially, however, your bird may be reluctant, as this is an unnatural action. Follow these steps to teach your conure to lay on his back:

- Start by getting him to perch on your finger.

- Then, rest your finger on a flat surface.

- Place the hand that is free on his back to support him and lean forward. Say, "on your back" or any such command in an excited voice. At one point he will be laying with his back on your hand.

- Now, shower him with praise and tell him how smart he is. You can give him toys and just play with him by tickling his tummy. He will learn to associate being on the back with positive experiences.

- You need to give him the same surface to practice all the time and lean forward a little.

- Then, the gesture of you leaning in also reinforces the habit and he will learn to lie down on his back.

While it does take some patience to teach your bird new tricks, it can be extremely fun and very fulfilling. It also gives you a chance to spend a lot of time with your bird. Of course, your conure will appreciate this immensely.

Chapter 6: Breeding Green Cheek Conures

When you buy a green cheek conure, it is a good idea to think about whether you want to breed them or not. If you can make up your mind initially, you can even buy your conures in pairs. That way, you can eliminate the process of introducing a mate to your conure.

That said, even if you decide to do so later on, you can follow a few simple rules and tips to make this phase a beautiful one. Conures breed readily in captivity. This is one of the reasons why there are so many hobby breeders. They also have interesting color mutations that make it even more challenging and exciting to breed them.

Green cheek conures become sexually mature at the age of about 2 years old. It can be earlier or later depending upon each individual bird. However, 2 years is the right time to introduce a mate to your bird if you have decided to breed them.

1. Introducing a mate to your conure

When you decide to introduce older birds to each other, the first thing to do is quarantine the new bird. Then, you must keep in mind that the female will be more aggressive and territorial than the male. These birds will dictate the whole relationship, the breeding season and also the rearing of the offspring.

So, if you have a female conure, the introduction must happen in a new and neutral environment where the female is less likely to be territorial. Follow the same steps mentioned in the earlier chapters about the introduction of two birds.

The next thing to do is to check whether the birds are showing any bonding behavior. The first sign is that the birds are feeding each other. If you do not see this behavior, you can give them wood that they can chew.

This is a part of the courtship ritual and you will eventually see them starting to feed one another. Only when you see this consistently should you provide a nesting box.

Never provide a nesting box before the birds have bonded. This will make the female hide in the nesting box all day and your birds will most likely not mate. Even if the birds do mate, the eggs that are laid are clear. They will not produce any chicks when they hatch.

Once the nesting box has been introduced after the birds have bonded, the male will initiate mating. During this phase you need to give the birds a larger portion of food. This will allow them to believe that they can provide for their young when they are born. Avoid touching the birds during this time. In addition, avoid loud music or any other stressful conditions for the birds.

In the first few days of introduction, you need to watch the birds extremely carefully. If you see that one of them is excessively aggressive towards the other, they may not be a compatible pair. Simply separate the birds. In case you are providing the bird with any supplement, be very cautious. If one of them is getting an overdose of the supplement, he or she may become aggressive and hyperactive, leading you to believe that the birds are not compatible while they may actually be the perfect pair.

2. Preparing for the breeding season

All birds require a warm and comfortable nesting box in order to initiate mating. You also need to make sure that your birds get the right nutrition to ensure healthy offspring.

Setting up the nesting box

You need to get a large nesting box that is at least 18 inches deep or more. This is basically to make sure that the nesting material, usually something soft like pine shavings, is available in plenty. Green cheek conures tend to keep kicking this material out and if the nest is not deep enough, there are chances that the amount of pine shavings available will not be enough when the eggs are laid.

You can use a wooden nesting box, however conures tend to be chewers and may damage the box, so a metal one is more suitable. The idea is to have a nesting box that can last for several breeding seasons. Conures prefer the same nesting box year after year.

This box can be placed at a high position in the cage. If you have a special nesting cage, you can place it there. Remember that height is an important factor for brooding hens to feel comfortable.

In case your bird does not have enough access to light, you may have to set up infrared lighting that you need to turn on at about 4 pm and turn off by about 10 pm.

The right diet for the breeding season

After mating, if the female spends most of her time in the nesting box, it only means that she is brooding. The diet of brooding conures should be really nutritious to avoid common problems such as egg binding, which can be very painful and sometimes fatal.

You need to give your conure fresh pellets, lots of fresh fruits and vegetables and even some cuttlebone to ensure that she has a good source of calcium. Ensuring that your conure is getting enough calcium can be a challenge but it is very important.

You can give them additional treats like raisins, almonds, walnuts, eggshells and even mineral blocks that are added to the water. Make sure that your bird gets good sunlight in order to utilize the calcium that you are providing her with.

Your vet should be able to help you with supplements that you can mix in the food or water of your conure.

Once the female has mated, she will begin to brood. You will know when she is ready to lay her eggs as she displays the following signs:

- Eating more from the mineral block or chewing from the cuttlebone.

- She will also become very cranky and noisy.

- Displaying territorial and aggressive behavior. The female will start seeking your attention and will want you to accept annoying behavior such as nipping at your shirt or biting. Do not encourage that.

- Development of a bald patch on the belly, which is called the brood patch. This is to help her pass heat from her body to the eggs.

When she is ready, she will lay the egg in the nesting box and will incubate it for about 28 days when provided with nesting conditions such as toys, sunlight and a lot of attention. Each clutch will have between 3 to 8 eggs. The hen lays one egg each day. It is possible that the first clutch is infertile. Conures are known for abandoning their clutch. If you see that your bird does not sit on the eggs and incubate them even after increasing the temperature, you will have to incubate the eggs artificially.

3. After the eggs have hatched

The biggest challenge that you will face is deciding between letting the birds parent the young ones or hand raising them yourself. If you allow the latter, the baby birds will develop better parenting instincts that will help breed them in the future. In the case of the latter, you will have birds that are friendlier and more accepting towards humans.

Most conure owners take the mid-road and co-parent the birds. This is ideal, as the baby birds get the best of both worlds.

Hand raising conures

If you decide to hand feed the baby birds, the ideal age to remove them from the cage is when they are about 3-4 weeks old. This is when the birds are in their pinfeather stage. Their feathers look like quills at this stage.

This is the best age as the birds are able to keep in body heat and will not require any artificial heat. These birds also have the advantage of being raised by their parents and will be healthier. Immunity is better, as the parents will pass on antibodies while feeding the babies.

Choose a formula recommended by your vet. Prepare the formula as per the instructions on the package. You need to make sure that the formula is heated to about 100 degrees F and not more than that. This can scald the insides of the delicate baby bird.

It is better to use a spoon to feed the baby as opposed to a syringe as you will be able to control the food going into the belly of the baby. That way you reduce the risk of choking the baby.

Feeding with a spoon is much slower, so chances of overfeeding are fewer. When the baby is full, you will be able to see the signs that will tell you when to stop feeding. You will also spend more time with the baby when you feed him with a spoon.

In case you pull the babies out of the nest earlier or have to hand feed them at an earlier stage because they were artificially incubated, you will have to purchase a brooder that will keep the babies warm as you feed them. The formula must be made very watery and should be given to the bird in small quantities. Then you wait for the crop to empty and feed the baby again. At a very young age, you may have to feed the baby every two hours.

At the pinfeather stage, you can feed the baby 4-5 times and give him some time to rest overnight. That way the crop will be fully empty and he will be ready for the next meal.

Co-parenting the baby birds

You may also choose to work with the conure parents and raise the chicks with them. This means that the conure parents will also be a part of the raising process. You will take turns between the feeding cycles and the babies will be removed from the nest to hand feed at least once a day.

Co-parenting is only possible when you have a very trusting relationship with your birds. If they can accept your attempts to take the babies out as assistance and not acceptance, then you can do this.

Your birds need to be extremely calm to allow you to co-parent the chicks. Otherwise they will develop aggressive behavior, which they will direct at each other. The male may attack the female or they may even kill the hatchlings. You must back off if the birds show any signs of resistance.

However, if the birds accept your assistance, it can be a wonderfully rewarding experience for you. The responsibility is reduced on your part and on the part of the conure parents, the babies are more social and tame, and the parents still have the pleasure raising their own young.

It does not matter how you choose to raise the birds. Remember that all the experiences are equally rewarding. You may choose to add these birds to your flock. That is, however, not a practical thing to do, as conures that have mated once will do so every year and the babies have a life span of about 30 years or more. So, it is a good idea to find these babies loving homes when they are a few years old.

Breeding conures is not for everyone, so make sure that you only do it if you are up for challenges such as the parents abandoning the nest within a few days of the eggs hatching.

In case you find the first experience with the chicks less exciting, you can discourage breeding by disallowing ideal nesting conditions as mentioned above. Some pet conure owners also avoid raising chicks because they find it very hard to give them away.

Weaning

During the hand-feeding period, you will have to keep the birds in warm boxes or bins. When they are ready to be weaned, they are also ready for the cages. Until then, they are too small for a cage.

You know that the bird is ready to be weaned when he starts handling small objects with his beak or tries to climb using the beak. You will now reduce the formula to twice a day and introduce the bird to eating on his own. Weaning basically means that you are getting the bird to a stage when he can eat on his own without your help or the parent's help.

Place the babies in a cage that is lined with newspaper. Place a feeding bowl and a water bowl in the cage. You need one for each chick and it should be shallow enough for the bird to eat from. It is recommended that you put the bird into this cage after hand feeding in the morning. If the birds are very hungry, they may refuse to eat on their own.

You will be able to attract the babies to the new food, preferably special baby pellets, by mixing in rice crispies. You will see that they do not mind experimenting as long as their tummy isn't fully empty. Eventually they will stop eating in the evening. Then they will slowly take to eating on their own and will wean with time. Never rush the baby. Prepare a feeding routine and stick to it and they will eventually learn to eat all their food.

Chapter 7: Travelling With Green Cheek Conures

There are many reasons why you may have to travel with your green check conures. To begin with, every trip to the vet will require you to take your bird on a drive.

While this may seem very easy to us, it is extremely unnatural and unsettling for the birds. So, it is extremely important to make sure that your bird feels comfortable and safe.

It is a bigger challenge when you have to cross borders with your pet bird. Whether you have to take him to another city, state or country, you need to make elaborate preparations. In some cases, you may have to leave the bird behind. Then, looking for someone reliable to take care of your bird is also necessary.

This chapter will tell you all you need to know about travelling with your birds.

1. Travelling by car

Getting your bird introduced to a car is a step-by-step process. It can demand a lot of patience from your end or it could be very easy to get your bird to love drives. It depends upon the personality of the bird and the measures you take to make this a positive experience for your bird.

- Get the bird used to the car. Just transfer him to a smaller traveling cage and place the cage in the car.

- Make sure that the air conditioning is on. It is not advisable to leave windows open when you are traveling with birds, as they may be stressed by drafts. If he shows discomfort, take him home. Try this until the bird is used to the car and remains calm inside.

- Initially, take short drives around the block. Give the bird plenty of water and food to keep him calm. Of course, water should be given through a bottle to prevent any spilling on the way.

- Make sure that the cage is lined with lots of substrate. You can also give your bird a toy to stay calm.

- Then drive slowly and keep talking to the bird. He may be scared and may retreat to one corner of the cage. This is natural. Keep the drive short and take him home. Do this until the bird is calm during these short trips.

- Now your bird is ready for a long drive. Prepare the cage with food, water and substrate. If you have any bags to take with you, introduce these bags during the short rides so that the bird can get used to the colors and shapes. Take breaks every half an hour to make sure that your bird is not stressed.

2. Travelling by air

Travelling by air is hard with any pet. With birds like the green cheek conure, their size makes them vulnerable to a lot of accidents. In addition to that, sudden changes in the environment and temperature can cause serious health issues.

It is best that you avoid air travel with conures as much as possible. However, if you have to make the move because you found a new job in another country or because you decided to settle down elsewhere, you need to ensure that air travel is completely safe and reliable.

- Check with the Fish and Wildlife Department of the place that you are traveling to about the restrictions with respect to conures. In some countries and states, you are not allowed to have these birds as pets. Others require you to obtain a permit or a license to bring your bird to their country.

- You can contact your local Wildlife Department to check about the procedure to obtain a permit. Usually, you will be able to get a permit within 60 days of application to the concerned authority.

- Once the permit is in place, you need to find an airline that has facilities to help you transport your bird safely.

- Read all the safety guidelines and provisions about livestock transport. Only when you are convinced should you opt for a certain airline. Make sure that all the transits are with the same airline to prevent any sudden changes in the rules and regulations.

- Obtain a travel cage as per the guidelines. Prepare the cage with water, food and substrate. In case of long flights, the airline will provide feeding services for your bird. Keeping him harnessed is a good idea to keep him safe.

- Having the wings clipped is a great option, as it will prevent any drama during the customs and security checks. The bird is easier to handle and the chances of escaping are lower when his wings have been clipped.

- Upon reaching your destination, have your bird examined by the vet. He may have symptoms of stress such as vomiting and dizziness because of the flight and the change in altitude. Immediate examination will make sure that he is safe.

- When you reach your new home, leave the bird in a quiet room with fresh water and food. Let him calm down and follow the same housebreaking procedure as mentioned above.

The laws of travelling overseas
There are several wildlife laws in order to protect certain species of animals. While green cheek conures are not considered endangered, there has been a steep decline in the wild populations of this bird. As a result, there may be several laws that make it hard for you to take the bird out of your country or even out of your state. There are three laws that you need to thoroughly check before you make any overseas plans involving the conure:
- Convention on the International Trade in Endangered Species of Wild Fauna and Flora (CITES)
- Wild Bird Conservation Act
- Endangered Species Act.

These laws have been enforced to ensure that these birds are safe and not illegally transported or traded. You can check the websites of these laws to see what laws are in reference to your conure. You may even take the assistance of your avian vet in determining whether traveling to certain countries is possible with conures or not. You may have to apply for special permits that will allow you to travel with your pet conure. It can take up to 60 days to process these permits, so you need to plan well in advance. You have to check these laws even if you are only crossing state borders.

3. Finding a good sitter

If you are only travelling temporarily on a vacation or for a business trip, taking your bird along is not recommended. It is a better idea to leave him in a place that is more familiar to him. This can be under the care of a relative, a pet sitter or even in a facility that may be provided by your own avian vet. For a temporary trip, it is not really worth putting your conure through so much stress.

Finding someone to care for your conure

The best option is to keep your conure in your home and request your friend or relative to take care of the bird. They should be entirely trustworthy. This is the best and most reliable option. However, if you do not have someone you know who can take care of your bird, you can always hire a pet sitter.

There are several professional pet sitters who can follow your routine and exact care while you are away. You can look in the yellow pages, ask fellow bird owners or check the Internet for options. Two of the most reliable sources to find pet sitters for your conure are National Association of Pet Sitters or www.petsitters.org and Pet Sitters International or www.petsit.com.

As per the National Association of Professional Pet Sitters, here are a few guidelines that you can follow to find a good pet sitter:

- Look for a sitter who has some commercial liability insurance. These are bonded sitters who can be held responsible in case something goes wrong with your pet.

- Make sure you have enough references from past clients. You can also ask the sitter to connect you with them. If there is any hesitation, you may want to reconsider.

- You need to get a complete written description of all the services that they will provide including the fees.

- You need to meet the pet sitter once. Ask them to visit your home and discuss all the services in complete detail.

- Be observant when you are interviewing the sitter. Is he comfortable with your conure?

- Ask him if he owns birds and also about the experience that he has with sitting for birds.

- You need to make a written contract in case you decide to use the services of a particular sitter. The most important thing is to check for his or her arrangements with veterinarians. In case your bird falls sick or there is any emergency, find out how he or she is going to deal with it.

- If the sitter herself or himself falls sick and is unable to care for your bird, is there any replacement? If so, meet that person.

In case you are not comfortable with the idea of leaving the bird with a sitter, there are several boarding options. The best one is with your avian vet if they provide those services. If not, you can ask them to recommend a suitable boarding house for your pet conure. Make sure you check the conditions of boarding and that your bird will be safe from any infections during this time.

Chapter 8: Health Issues With Green Cheek Conures

Like all species of parrots, green cheek conures are at a risk of contracting several diseases. These diseases are usually the result of nutritional deficiencies while others are stress induced. The first thing to do is to identify that your bird is unwell. Here are some sure shot signs that your green cheek conure is unwell:

- Resting too often
- Poor appetite
- Opening and closing the beak frequently
- Sticking to the bottom of the cage
- Reduced water intake or sudden increase in water intake
- Growth around the beak
- Loose droppings
- Sudden weight loss with the chest bone becoming more prominent
- Cloudy eyes
- Discharge from the eyes and nasal cavity
- Ruffled feathers
- Lethargy
- Drooping wings.

If you see these signs you should take your bird to the vet immediately as a preventive measure against impending health problems that can be serious.

It is important not to panic, as these symptoms may have other causes too. For instance, if the droppings are loose and dark colored, it could be the result of eating a particular food or veggie. However, taking the bird to a vet is a good preventive measure.

1. Common Health Issues

With most birds, diseases are airborne, so all the precautions that you may take to keep your bird healthy and free from illnesses may not seem good enough. Staying updated about conure health and diseases will help you be prepared for any emergency. Here are some of the most common health conditions observed in green cheek conures:

Pacheco Virus Disease

What is it?

- This is highly contagious disease.
- It is caused by a type of herpes virus that is found in South America. This is one of the top causes of conure deaths.

Symptoms:
- Quick liver damage that can even kill the bird.
- Bright colored vomit that is usually green or yellow.
- Symptoms are very mild and almost not noticeable initially.
- In the advanced stages, you will see neurological symptoms.

In many cases, birds could just be carriers of this virus. That is why quarantining new members of the flock is very important.

Remedy:

- Administer Acyclovir every 8 hours.
- This medicine is very expensive and is most often detested by birds.
- In case of Pacheco's disease, the progress is so rapid that most treatments are not effective.

Beak and Feather Syndrome (PBFDS)

What is it?

- This condition is mainly spread by dried droppings and feather dust.
- The condition, when allowed to progress, can be fatal.

Symptoms

- You will notice abnormal development of new feathers.
- The feathers that develop after molting will appear really swollen and messy.

- The beak looks very dull and covered in feather dust. Normally, the beak has a distinct shine.
- Abnormal growth of the beak.
- If allowed to progress, PBFDS can lead to paralysis.

Remedy:

- There is no exact cure.
- In conures, PBFD will eventually cause death.
- Sometimes, the birds are also put to sleep.
- Isolating affected birds will protect the rest of the flock.
- In some cases, it is possible for the birds to develop immunity naturally over a period of time. Then, bird goes back to normal and has no symptoms. This is possible with continued care and good nutrition.

Wasting Disease

What is it?

- This is a disease that affects all species of conures.
- It is a viral infection that manifests suddenly.
- It is very contagious and can go unnoticed or stay dormant for several years.
- This impact is primarily on the nervous system of your bird.

Symptoms:

- Tremors.
- Paralysis.
- Seizures.
- Cardiac arrests that are fatal to the birds.

Remedy:

- There is no cure for this condition.
- When your bird has been diagnosed with this condition, adding lots of supplementation in his food can prolong his life.
- The best supplements are ones that can be digested easily by your bird.

- In many cases, the final outcome of this condition is death of the bird as there are no preventive measures.

Papilloma

What is it?

- This is yet another viral infection but the good news is that it is not fatal.

Symptoms:

- You will see signs of infection near the mouth and the throat of the bird.
- You will see a wart-like growth that develops in this region.
- You need to have these removed immediately.
- While the infection itself is not fatal, the growths can block the nasal passage or the throat and cause death by choking.
- The growth keeps increasing in size, leading to several physiological conditions if not treated on time.

Remedy:

- The best remedy for this condition is to have the infected area treated. The growth can be removed using a laser surgery.

Psittacosis

What is it?

- Also known as conure fever, this is a viral infection.
- The younger ones are more susceptible.
- They have a less mature the immune system and are at a higher risk of infection.
- This condition is caused by a strain of the chlamydiosis virus.

Symptoms:

- Pneumonia
- Conjunctivitis
- Nasal discharge
- Incessant sneezing

- Lime green droppings
- Liver and kidney malfunction
- Seizures
- Tremors
- Paralysis
- Neurological issues.

Remedy:

- Administering tetracycline or doxycycline.
- Administer medication through an injection or orally.
- A normal course of this medicine lasts for 45 days.
- Keep the cage sanitized.

Remember that this condition is also contagious to human beings, leading to pneumonia or fever. Make sure you wash your hands every time you handle the bird or its belongings. You can even wear a mask while doing so.

Gout

What is it?

- Any calcification in the kidney leads to gout.
- Common in younger birds that are around 4 - 8 weeks of age.
- Caused by an imbalance of calcium in the food. This condition can occur in birds that have a lower metabolism, as it is related mostly to the diet.

Symptoms:

- Slight dehydration
- Vomiting
- The skin on the chest shrinks
- The bird is unable to retain fluids and food.

These initial signs are similar to any bacterial infection. However, getting a blood test done when you see these symptoms is advised.

Remedy

- The birds should be kept hydrated always.

- Colchicine and Allopurinal are recommended to flush out the urates from the bird's body.

Conure Pox

What is it?

- All species of conures are susceptible to this condition.
- Caused by an avian pox virus infection.
- Infection can be spread by insects.
- They are also contagious and can be spread from one bird to another.

Symptoms:

- Discharge from the mouth, eyes and gullet.
- Depigmentation.
- Abnormalities in the roof of the beak.
- Depression.
- Scars will compromise the appearance of the bird.

Remedy:

- Provide the bird with high amounts of Vitamin A.
- Injecting vitamins is preferred.
- Antibiotics will be administered by the vet.
- Force-feed the bird if he stops eating to get the best results. Sometimes, he just may be too weak to eat.
- Mucous in the eyes or nasal passage must be cleaned using a prescribed washing solution. Otherwise, these deposits will harden and cause damage to the body parts. Allow the scabs to stay once they have formed to protect your conure.

Aspergillosis

What is it?

- This is a condition that affects the lungs of the bird.
- Aspergillosis is caused by the Aspergella fungus.
- This fungus usually thrives in dark and damp areas.
- Poor sanitation is a prime cause of this condition.

Symptoms:

- Cough
- Fever
- Chest pain
- Dysponea
- Anorexia
- Strained breathing
- Lethargy
- White colored mucous
- Depression in the birds. If the central nervous system is affected, it leads to paralysis.
- Sudden death.

Remedy:

- Administatrion of intraconozole and fluconazole.
- Ensure better sanitation to improve the response to medication.

Salmonellosis

What is it?

- This is one of the most serious infections in birds.
- Most birds are carriers of these bacteria.
- In most cases, infected birds are put to sleep, as they pose a great threat to other birds in the aviary.
- However, even in the acute stages, this condition can be treated.

Symptoms:

- Droopiness
- Diarrhea
- Severe lethargy
- Chronically ill birds are emaciated.
- Birds in the last stage of the disease often have seizures.

Remedy:

- Screen every bird for infection.

- If one of the conures is diagnosed with salmonellosis, make sure he is kept isolated.
- This is the best way prevent the infection from spreading.
- Administer antibiotics when the bird is in isolation.

Salmonella can cause serious infections in humans too. If you have birds of any kind at home, all members of your family must wash their hands thoroughly before eating. It is recommended that you wash your hands immediately after handling the birds.

Sinusitis

What is it?

- In most species of conures, this is a very common respiratory problem.
- When you bring home a green cheek conure, ensure you always have the medicines for cold and any respiratory infection within easy access.
- The cause of this condition is unknown.
- It is very contagious and requires immediate attention.
- One organism that is suspected to cause this condition in birds is mycoplasma, although there is no confirmation for this.

Symptoms:
- Nasal discharge.
- Swollen eyes.
- Sneezing.
- Cold symptoms.

Remedy:

- Sinusitis is followed by secondary infections, usually making treatment complicated.
- The best way to control this condition is by providing high doses of Vitamin A. If the bird does not respond to this, consult your vet.

Nasal Discharge

What is it?

- This is very common in all species of conures who are not getting enough Vitamin A in their diet.
- You can reduce the symptoms of this condition by increasing supplementation and by increasing the quantity of food. It is very important to give your green cheek conure a balanced diet to prevent any health problem.

Conure Bleeding Syndrome

What is it?

- This is another disease that is commonly seen in green cheek conures.
- It is believed to be caused by a certain strain of retrovirus, although the exact cause remains unknown.
- Another theory is that this condition is caused by vitamin K deficiency.
- If left untreated, this condition may be fatal for conures.

Symptoms:

- The initial symptoms are very similar to heavy metal poisoning.
- Discomfort .
- Uncharacteristic screaming.
- The most significant symptom is bleeding from the mouth and nasal cavity.

Remedy:
- Injecting Vitamin D3 and K1 are the most effective remedies for this condition in green cheek conures.

2. Preventive Measures

Disease prevention in pets is only a matter of establishing a healthy environment for them. Some of the best preventive measures include:

- Quarantining new birds to ensure that there are no contagious diseases.

- Providing a balanced meal that is rich in vitamins, especially vitamin A and minerals like calcium.

- Making sure that clean drinking water is available to the bird at all times.

- Give him a lot of mental stimulation through toys and games. Green cheek conures need a lot of attention.

- Make sure that he has access to enough sunlight and maybe full spectrum sunlight every day. Take them out into the porch and let them soak the sun in for a while.

- Keeping the cage, food and water bowls clean.

- Grooming the bird and keeping him clean.

- Regular visits to the veterinarian. It is recommended that you have your bird checked every 6 months to 1 year.

With all these preventive measures, you should be able to prevent most infections and illnesses that may affect your green cheek conures.

3. Dealing With Common Injuries

Your bird is susceptible to several accidents at home or even because of some aggression among the flock. You need to be prepared to take care of the most common injuries that are seen among pet birds.

Here are some of the most common problems that you are likely to face with your green cheek conure:

Broken blood feathers

When a blood feather breaks, it will bleed profusely. Here are some measures you can take in the case of a broken blood feather:

- You need to make sure that you pack the shaft with flour or styptic powder.

- You will get a styptic pencil in your local super market.

94

- You must cover this with gauze and press it gently.

- Then take your bird to the vet to have the shaft removed. With experience, you will learn to remove this shaft yourself.

Animal attack

If you have a cat or a dog at home and your bird has been attacked, you need to make sure that your bird gets first aid immediately. These are the measures you should take:

- The first thing that you will do is calm the bird down, if the bird is not seriously injured.

- Shift him to a calm and quiet place and let him settle down. Then, examine the wounds.

- Any bleeding should be stopped using gauze. DO NOT use the styptic pencil in this case.

- If you notice that the wing is broken, hold it close to the body and tie it loosely using the gauze.

- Then, rush your pet to the vet immediately. Remember, the mouth of a cat or dog carries several bacteria that can be toxic for a bird, so every wound needs to be examined immediately.

Burns

In case your bird has an accidental burn by sitting on a hot stove or brushing against a hot container, you need to take the following steps:

- Run cold water on the area that is affected for a while.

- Then, dab the area dry using clean gauze.

- A cold compress can be applied to the area to provide immediate relief. A severe burn needs immediate veterinary care, as the bird may be very stressed.

- You may have to provide certain antibiotics to ensure that there is no infection.

Poisoning

Poisoning can occur for several reasons. The bird may inhale the toxic fumes from a teflon pan, ingest something poisonous or even come into contact with metals like lead and zinc. You will notice that your bird's beak is wide open, along with labored breathing and rapid wagging of the tail. If the bird has inhaled or ingested the toxin, make sure you do the following:

- Call your vet immediately.

- Alternatively, you can call the **ASPCA National Animal Poison Control Center** on 888-4ANI-HELP (888-426-4435). They will want exact details about the type of toxin involved, the weight of your bird, when the exposure occurred and the symptoms that your bird is showing.

- If you see that his eyes have been affected by the toxin, the eyes need to be washed before you take the bird to a vet.

4. Conure First Aid Kit

Any evident injury needs professional care. However, you need to have a first aid kit to help provide immediate relief to your conure. Some essentials in the first aid kit are:

- Flour: This is very effective in controlling bleeding without increasing blood pressure.
- File: To keep the beak and nails trimmed.
- Tweezers: Usually bird bandages and tapes are tiny and need tweezers to hold them easily.
- Cotton swabs: To control any bleeding and to clean any pus or blood off the bird.
- Gauze: Use sterile ones to stop bleeding in open wounds.
- Bandage material: To control bleeding, hold the wing in place when it is broken. Make sure that you get bandage that won't stick to the conure's feathers.
- Toothpick: To remove any debris in the nostrils.

- Disinfectant: Hydrogen peroxide is the best option to clean a wound. This is the only thing you can use without the vet's recommendation as long as you keep it away from the eyes, mouth and ears.
- A small syringe: this will help you wash off the wounds.
- A towel: To restrain an injured bird.

This is the basic kit that you must always keep handy to ensure that you are able to provide immediate medical help to your green cheek conures whenever necessary.

5. Finding the best avian vet

The most important part of good healthcare for your green cheek conure is finding the perfect avian vet. Avian vets specialize in treating birds. While a general vet can take care of emergencies, you will need an avian vet for the more bird-specific health issues.

Their practice also includes several hours of work with facilities that deal especially with birds. Most avian vets are members of the Association of Avian Vets. If you can find one who is a member, it is great. However, you could even have an avian vet who is not a part of it because he or she has not worked with birds that are of a very rare species.

It is convenient if your breeder can recommend a good avian vet. However, if you feel like you need more options because this clinic is inaccessible or you are are not satisfied with the facility, you may even ask for details in a local bird club, an online bird forum, a pet store or even in the clinic of a vet dealing with animals like cats and dogs. One reliable source to find all the contact details of avian vets from across the country is the Association of Avian Vets. You can visit their website www.aav.org or call their central office in Florida on 407-393-8901. Once you have the details, make sure you personally visit the clinic to ensure that your bird will be in safe hands.

Questions to ask the avian vet

You need to ask the avian vet that you have chosen a few important questions. This will give you a fair idea about the experience and the commitment of the facility towards the well being of your bird. Remember, you need to be able to sustain the relationship with your

97

avian vet for a really long time. So, find someone who is compatible and approachable. Here are a few questions that you can ask the vet during the interview:

Do they treat only birds?

Sometimes, avian vets may also tend to other species of animals that are exotic. This includes reptiles and a few rodents too. In that case, find out how much of the practice is dedicated to birds. If the vet is only taking care of 3-4 birds in a week or month, then you may have to look for more options, as the facility may not specialize in birds.

How do they stay updated?

Avian medicine is a fast changing field. One needs to stay updated by attending seminars, reading journals, etc. Ask your vet if s/he is associated with any club or if s/he attends any conference or seminar regularly. Ask them with an intention of participating in one yourself. If your vet is willing to take time off to learn about the birds, s/he is certainly committed to providing the best care for your bird.

How experienced is the staff?

You should be able to guess this by the behavior of the staff members towards you and your bird. If they are uncomfortable handling the cage or the bird, they are definitely not experienced. You need to make sure that everyone, including the front office, is friendly towards the birds.

How much time does each appointment last?

This will help you decide if the vet is thorough in the examination or not. If you are only going to get 15-20 minutes, it means that the facility is not up to the mark. They need to get the bird out of the cage and perform a thorough check up. That is when you know for sure that they are doing a good job. This will take at least 30-45 minutes per bird.

Is s/he available 24/7?

Emergencies never give you a warning, so you need to know some way of accessing medical assistance 24/7. If your vet does not have such a facility, s/he will at least be associated with one that is good and reliable.

Do they have hostels to admit the bird?

Ask them how they would care for a bird that needs to be admitted, probably post surgery. They should be associated with some hostel that helps them with this. Of course, some facilities have their own little wards for the birds. Make sure that the birds are kept in individual cages in clean and hygienic conditions.

Know when to walk out
If you observe one or more of the following signs, you need to try and find a new facility for your bird:

- The staff is unable to provide you with any instructions over the phone in case of an emergency. They will not even be able to provide advice about brining your bird to the vet when it is too cold or too hot outside.

- The staff members do not know how to handle birds.

- Weighing the birds is not a regular practice when you take them in for a checkup.

- The vet examines the bird whilst in the cage.

- Diet is not an important subject of discussion when your bird is unwell.

- They do not have basic facilities such as incubators or gram scales.

Once you have found a vet who is reliable, you must ensure that your bird is taken for regular check ups and is kept in the best of health.

Chapter 9: Expenses With Green Cheek Conures

Now that you are aware of all the care that your conure needs, let us take a look at the monetary responsibility that you will be taking on by bringing a conure home.

- Cost of the Conure: $200 - 400 or £100 - 250 depending upon the age, the breeding conditions and the source that you buy them from.

- Cage: $150 - 400 or £80 - 200 depending on the features available and the size. This is a one-time investment and it is recommended that you get the best.

- Food: $40 or £25 every month.

- Toys: This really depends upon the type of toys that you buy, but you will shell out a minimum of $15 or £10 on each toy that you buy.

- Wing clipping: If you get a wing clipped by someone else, then you will spend about $15 to £10 every four months.

- Veterinarian Cost: You will spend at least $50 or £30 per visit to your veterinarian. You can expect annual costs of about $1200 or £650.

- Pet Insurance: Depending on the kind of cover that you are getting, your pet insurance may cost anything between $150 - 280 or £80 - 150 every month.

Make sure your budget is in place before you bring the conure home. Be very sure that you can afford to take care of the bird, as the costs will be ongoing for 20-30 years.

Conclusion

Thank you for choosing this book. The goal of this book is to help you understand the behavior and the requirements of green cheek conures. Hopefully, you have found ample information to understand what your bird needs and if the conure is, indeed, the perfect addition to your family.

If you have had any questions about raising conures and this book has been able to answer them, then I consider my job done. It is the objective of this book to ensure that you can have a beautiful journey with your bird. The health and well being of pet conures is the primary objective of this book.

Before you can bring home a conure ask yourself these questions:

- Are you comfortable with some noise in your household from time to time? Yes
- Do you have some time to spare each day for your bird? Yes
- Can you take care of all the expenses related to the bird? Yes
- Is your home environment suited for the bird? Yes
- Will you be able to spend some time to prepare your family, especially children, to treat the birds properly? Yes

Once you have the answer to all these questions, you are ready to become a proud green cheek conure parent.

References

There is no end to how much you can learn about your green cheek conure. The more you learn, the better prepared you are for any challenges that you may face along the way when you are raising your beloved pet.

Note: at the time of printing, all the websites below were working. As the internet changes rapidly, some sites might no longer be live when you read this book. That is, of course, out of our control.

The Internet is one of the best sources to stay updated about the requirements of your conure. Here are some reliable sources that you can refer to when you want more information:

www.gcch.tripod.com

www.greencheekconure.net

www.animalspot.net

www.petgreencheekconure.com

www.greencheekedconure.blogspot.com

www.northernparrots.com

www.parrot-and-conure-world.com

www.blog.parrotessentials.co.uk

www.gccmadcap.blogspot.com

www.myconure.com

www.forums.avianavenue.com

www.birdtricks.com

www.caiquesite.com

www.shadypines.com

www.beautyofbirds.com

www.adoptapet.com

www.betterwords.typepad.com

www.petsuppliesplus.com

www.oldworldaviaries.com

www.parrotsecrets.com

www.animals.mom.me.com

www.templeaviaries.com

www.sciencedirect.com

www.parrotparrot.com

www.lafeber.com

www.onegreenplanet.org/

www.featherme.com

www.companionparrots.org

www.merckvetmanual.com/

www.peteducation.com/

Printed in Great Britain
by Amazon